English & Culture in Tourism

Australia, New Zealand, Canada, U.S.A., Guam, Hawaii and the Northern Mariana Island

Myeung-hee Seong
Hyung-ji Chang

English & Culture in Tourism

Myeong Hee Seong
Hyung-ji Chang

2007년 2월 26일 인 쇄
2007년 3월 2일 발 행

저자 / 성명희 · 장형지
발행인 / 진 욱 상
발행처 / 백산출판사
등록 : 1974. 1. 9. 제1-72호
서울시 성북구 정릉3동 653-40
전화 : (02)914-1621, 917-6240
팩스 : (02)912-4438

www.baek-san.com
edit@baek-san.com

ISBN 978-89-7739-939-6 92740

Preface

This book is mainly concerned about the field of Tourism, where most instructors are struggling because of limitation of English or knowledge of the tourism. Most of Tourism departments are instructed by professors both of English and Tourism majors. Thus this book suggests the methodological approach how to teach English in the field of tourism in terms of ESP (English for Specific Purpose) as well as Content-based Instruction. The predominant point of this book is the part of Culture, whichfacilitates the languageacquisition, combining knowledge with language under the category of Tourism. Even though this book is not fully enough to cover all the details of Tourism, it will be a fundamentaldirection that helps to teach English in Tourism.

The content of this book is covering mostly English speaking countries, where most of the famous tourist attractions are located in the world. The first chapter startswith Australia, the popular destination among tourists, and the second chapter is about New Zealand, the paradise of extreme sports lovers. The third chapter is about Canada, where nature and civilization are living together, and then the fourth to the last chapter is about the United States of America starting from the American continent to Pacific Islands; Mainland in America, Guam, Hawaii, and the Northern Mariana Islands, where people have experienced the exotic flavors with the indigenous people. In addition, each chapter consists of grammar focus, vocabulary preview, comprehension check, discussion questions and tips for travelers. The discussion questions provide the opportunities for students to share and expand their experiences with peers, accelerating more communicative competence. On top of that, the tips for travelers give the authentic information for university students as well as actual travelers.

In short, the book, English and Culture in Tourism is for both instructors and learners who are planning to be an expert in Tourism, informing the authentic culture and language of favorable countries in the world. As an author of this book, dare wish that this book can the keynote in Tourism English.

Contents

Chapter 3. *Canada*

Chapter 4. *United States of America*

Chapter 5 *Pacific Island I*

Chapter 6 *Pacific Island II*

English & Culture in Tourism

Australia
New Zealand
Canada
U.S.A.
Guam
Hawaii
the Northern Mariana Island

Chapter 1
Australia

Chapter 1

Australia

GETTING STARTED...

Location	Oceania, continent between the Indian Ocean and the South Pacific Ocean
Climate	Generally arid to semiarid; temperate in south and east; tropical in north
Population	20,090,437
Ethnic group	Caucasian 92%, Asian 7%, aboriginal and other 1%
Religions	Catholic 26.4%, Anglican 20.5%, other Christian 20.5%, Buddhist 1.9%, Muslim 1.5%, other 1.2%, unspecified 12.7%, none 15.3%
Languages	English 79.1%, Chinese 2.1%, Italian 1.9%, other 11.1%, unspecified 5.8%

Harbor Bridge, Sydney

UNIT 1

About Australia

Grammar focus

1. **Numbering**

Ordinal numbers always come with an article, 'the'.

the first, the second, the third, the fourth, the fifth···

2. **An article, the**

'The' places with the superlative

the largest, the lowest, the prettiest, the longest···

3. **Preposition**

Preposition to **follows** from

From Seoul to Pusan

4. **A correlative conjunction**

Not only A but (also) B

Not only English, but also Korean

Vocabulary

population	density	authentic	aboriginal
traditional	civilization	climate	continent
destination	temperature	accommodation	quantity
quality	particular	fiber	retail
yield	private	comfortable	

Australia is the sixth largest country in the world. It's about the same size as the 48 mainland states of the USA and 50 percent larger than Europe, but has the lowest population density in the world - only two people per square kilometers.

There is a large variety of authentic Aboriginal art for sale or viewing. From traditional dot and bark paintings, modern 'earth pigment' screen prints, decorated jewelry and wood carvings, to boomerangs, didgeridoos, weapons, ceramics, scarves, even compact discs with traditional music. In whatever form it takes, the art of this amazing civilization should not be missed on the visit.

Australia's climate and the fact that it is the driest continent on earth make it a fabulous holiday destination all year round. During winter, you can ski in the southern states one day and be diving in the balmy waters of the Great Barrier Reef in Queensland the next. Such temperate conditions make open air dining, great days on the beach or the water, outdoor barbeques, and a huge variety of sports a way of life here. No wonder Australians believe life is for living.

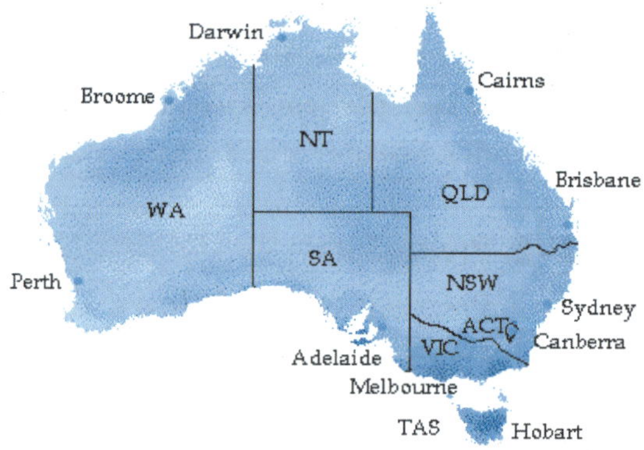

Map of Australia

Australia is known not only for its quantity of sheep, but the quality of wool they produce. Merino in particular produces the longest wool fibers in the world. Australian designers have taken this remarkable wool and produced spectacular clothing including hand-knitted sweaters and jackets that are the envy of the world. As well as clothing, beautiful soft blankets and bedding are also available. When buying these products, always look for the Pure New Wool label to guarantee their quality. Australian merino wool is not to be missed and is available in most department stores and retail outlets.

Getting to Australia is easy. There is a range of regularly scheduled flights to Australia, offering the chance to fly direct or to take advantage of the many stopover destinations on offer.

You can expect the highest standards of accommodation in a range designed to suit every budget. Make your choice from luxury hotels and resorts, comfortable motels, apartments and hostels, to farms and private homes.

Skyline of Sydney

Comprehension Check

1. Australia is the ( ) largest country in the world.
2. There is an enormous variety of authentic ( ) art for sale and viewing.
3. Australia is the ( ) continent on earth.
4. Australia is known not only for its quantity of sheep, but the quality of ( ) they produce.
5. ( ) is not to be missed and is available in most department store and retail outlets.

Discussion Questions

1. Have you ever been to Australia? If so, How was your first impression when you arrived at the country?
2. If you had a chance to live in Australia, where would you like to stay? Would you like to stay in a city like Sydney or the outback with kangaroos?
3. What types of transportation will you choose to travel around Australia?
4. Which season do you prefer to visit Australia? Summer or winter?
5. If you go to Australia during the vacation, are you going to take a direct plane or a stopover one?

Useful Conversation

▣ When you travel, you will make a travel plan in the travel agency.

A : I'd like to go to Australia.

B : Where would you like to go in Australia?

A : I'd like to go to Sydney. I'm going to stay there for a week.

B : We have many kinds of flights, what day would you like to leave?

A : Well, I'd like to leave on December 20th.

B : First class or economy class?

A : Economy class, please, which airline is the most economical?

B : Australian airline is not too expensive and comfortable. But you have to transfer the flight at Narita airport in Japan, and it takes about an hour.

A : How much does it cost if I take Korean Airline?

B : It's about $2000 for round trip.

A : How about Australian Airline?

B : It costs $1000 for round trip.

A : Well, I'll take Australian Airline then.

B : Thank you very much, and let me book your flight.

UNIT 2 Tourist Attractions

Grammar focus

1. The patterns of sentence

S+V	A great number of people go there.
S+V+C	The reef is invaluable to scientist.
S+V+O	It poses a challenge to seekers.
S+V+IO+DO	Their unearthly beauty brings travelers the poem.
S+V+O+OC	The Opera House makes a lot of audience crowded every year.

2. Subject and verb agreement.

One of Plural Noun + Plural Verb

One of the World's performing arts centers are ~

Vocabulary

bewitch	incredibly	challenge
adventure	ancestral	unearthly
rustic	unique	wonders
coral	reef	heritage
encompass	facility	exclusive
contemporary	capacity	adequate
preserve	abundant	

2.1 Unique wonders of the desert

Uluru (Ayers Rock) has attracted travelers from all over the world. Sitting in the heart of Australia, it rises 348 meters from the ground. Incredibly, that's only a third of it, the remainder submerges underneath the Earth's surface.

Ayers Rock

It poses a challenge to seekers of mystery and adventure everywhere. What formed this solitary red rock? What secrets does it hide? The Anangu, aboriginal people, who respect this rock as a mother, know many of the answers, and their understanding and legends of this beautiful land can do much to open the travelers' eyes. They can take you on a walking tour around the rock's mighty feet, sharing stories out of their ancestral culture and introducing you to the wildlife that is linked to the Anangu legends of Uluru.

Just half an hour away is Kata Tjuta (Mt. Olgas), meaning many heads. These are a collection of 36 stunning red, stone-shaped monoliths, covering an area of 3,500 hectares. Some are 250 meters higher than Uluru, with the tallest, Mt Olga, rising 546 meters tall.

Both Uluru and Kata Tjuta respond wonderfully to the shifting light and times of the day. Their unearthly beauty brings out many poets in the most travelers. Together they form the Uluru-Kata Tjuta National Park, which is a sacred site of the Anangu people.

Accommodation in and around the Park offers lodgings from the most rural to the highest degree of comfort. Here you can stay as long as you need to truly appreciate these unique wonders.

2.2 A Coral Wonderland

The Great Barrier Reef is more than just a scene of incomparable natural beauty lying beneath clear blue waters. World Heritage listed that it encompasses more than 1000 islands and 2,900 individual reefs, and shelters 1,500 species of fish and 400 species of coral. It is unimaginably vast, stretching more than 2000 kilometers - more than the total combined surface area of the United Kingdom and Ireland.

The reef is fascinating to children, invaluable to scientists, and irresistible to seekers of paradise. Many isles are covered with lush and undisturbed rainforests.

The Great Barrier Reef

A good number of the reef's islands are open to visitors and have comfortable island resorts or camping facilities. Others lie invitingly to be explored by boat. The trick is to find the island that best suits your preferences. If you wish to stay in an exclusive resort, there is beautiful Orpheus Island beckons. Or try the eco-cabins at Double Island, or Green Island which has one of the most luxurious resorts in the world, or Haggle stone, so exclusive it is only open for some months of the year.

Many grades of accommodation in beautiful surroundings can be found throughout the islands. Try Hinchinbrook Island, the world's largest island national park, Whitsunday Island, where the fine white sands and warm blue water are legendary, lizard Island, for superb game fishing and scuba-diving, or sensational Dunk Island.

2.3 Sydney Opera House

Sydney Opera House

Sydney Opera House, an extraordinary structure on the harbor at Bennelong Point, is one of the world's premier performing-arts centers. Opened in 1973, it has taken its place among the world's most important buildings. It was designed by a Danish architect Jorn Utzon and took almost 15 years to build.

Sydney Opera House is more than just a venue, it is home to the Australian performing arts scene and a place where outstanding art is created and presented by extraordinary artists from around the world. Sydney Opera House is a place where the spirit and imagination of the community is brought to life through the innovative arts programs.

The magnificent sail-like structure houses a complex of almost 1,000 rooms and many different performance spaces, halls and theatres. The Opera House has the capacity to produce a range of entertainment from classical to contemporary. In an average year, it presents theater, musicals, opera, contemporary dance, ballet, and all sorts of different musical forms from symphony concerts to jazz, exhibitions and films. Open-air concerts have even taken place on its steps. It averages around 3,000 events each year, with audiences totaling up to two million per year.

A great many people also go there just for the sake of the building. Countless people jump off the train at East Circular Quay and walk up to the Opera House just to take a photograph on its steps, and around 200,000 people take guided tours of the building each year. Even the path to the Opera House, along Bennelong Point, is dotted with artists and all kinds of street theater. Since opening in 1973, the Sydney Opera House is now one of the busiest performing arts centers and attracts talent from all over the world.

2.4 Kangaroo Island

Kangaroo Island, near the tip of South Australia's Fleurieu Peninsula, is Australia's third largest island. Civilization and wilderness meet there in harmony, and sea lions, penguins, dolphins, koalas and kangaroos live in the natural environment.

Kangaroo Island

Kangaroo Island has a wild, untouched beauty that has been preserved from overdevelopment and excessive tourism. Original flora and fauna remain abundant, cliffs and beaches are unsullied, and many roads are left unreached.

The best place in Australia to view sea lions, Seal Bay Conservation Park in South Australia, is home to a population of up to 600 sea lions. They can be seen up close, lolling about in the sun, nursing pups, or diving into the ocean for fish.

Flinders Chase National Park is a wilderness and wildlife haven on the south-western tip of Kangaroo Island, and is known for its woodland and stunning coastline.

2.5 The Gold Coast

The Gold Coast packs several destinations in one. This region has places for swimming, a cluster of theme parks featuring anything from dolphins to film-making, open air and waterfront dining, a busy nightlife and more shopping per square kilometer than anywhere in Australia.

The Gold Coast is bounded by historic Beenleigh to the north and Cabarita Beach - just over the New South Wales border - to the south. 70 kilometers of coastline includes spectacular South Stradbroke Island, and a string of vibrant beachside areas. The stretch's 35 patrolled beaches include Surfer's Paradise, Broad Beach, and Main Beach, known for their surfing and swimming opportunities.

Gold Coast

A game of golf isn't hard to find on the Gold Coast, which has 40 resort and championship golf courses. If you're more interested in unique animals, the Gold Coast is still the best place to feed native birds and to cuddle a koala.

Just 30 minutes' drive from the beaches is the Hinterland, Australia's largest reserve of subtropical rainforest, with 160 kilometers of walking tracks, and Springbrook and Tamborine national parks. You'll find stunning scenes of waterfalls, and rare flora and fauna. You can drive for the camping and adventures, or climb in the mountain and explore rainforest hideaways.

The Gold Coast offers accommodation to suit every budget, with a collection of luxury hotels, rainforest retreats, serviced and self-contained apartments, family camp sites and motels, tourist parks and hostels, bed-and-breakfast and farm stay accommodations.

Comprehension Check

1. Sitting in the heart of Australia, Ayers Rock rises (   ) meters from the ground.
2. The Great Barrier Reef encompasses more than 1000 (   ) and 2,900 individual (   ).
3. The Opera House has the capacity to produce a range of entertainment from (   ) to the (   ).
4. Kangaroo Island is Australia's third (   ) island.
5. This region has places for swimming, a cluster of theme parks featuring anything from (   ) to (   ).

Discussion Questions

1. Where is the Ayers Rock? What is the meaning of the Ayers Rock for Australians?
2. Which attraction is the well known symbol of Australia?
3. What types of performances can people see in the Opera House?
4. If you were in Australia which place would you want to visit the most?

Useful Conversation

■ When you travel, you have to make a reservation for a hotel

A : Good morning, Reservation Desk, Kim speaking. May I help you?

B : Yes, I'd like to reserve a room.

A : When would you like the room for, sir?

B : From December 20th to 22nd,

A : What kind of room would you like, sir?

B : A double with bath.

A : Would you like a room in the front or the back of the hotel?

B : In the front, please?

A : May I have your name please?

B : Yes, my name is Stanley Gold.

A : Would you spell your name, please?

B : S-T-A-N-L-E-Y.

A : Very good, sir. We have a package with a complementary breakfast.

B : That's very good, I'll take it.

A : We'll see you on December 20th.
Thank you very much for calling.

B : Thank you, bye.

UNIT 3 Things to do

3.1 Amazing Experiences

Whale Watching

Australia is a land full of powerful experiences just waiting to be discovered. Encounters with incredible wildlife on land and in the water will truly open the eyes wide in astonishment. And as well as adventures for adrenaline seekers there are plenty that everyone can enjoy.

The experience of seeing the gigantic creatures rising from the ocean is unforgettable. Many coastal towns offer boat or flight seeing trips as well as beach or cliff top viewing areas.

Climb Sydney's Bridge

Harbor Bridge

Climbing Sydney's Harbor Bridge offers picturesque view, one of the most spectacular harbor views on the planet. Drink in the drama of sparkling sapphire water against the white sails of the Opera House below you, and you can breathe the fresh and clean air.

Pat a Koala

One of the most memorable experiences you can have is to cuddle a koala. At the wildlife parks within easy reach of several major cities you can hold, feed and photograph these cute and fascinating creatures.

3.2 Food and Dining

Markets on street

Fine wines and dining are as warm as sun and booming waves to Australians. Wherever your travels take you, just as the sights and sounds of marvelous landscapes will live on in your memory, its food and wine will resonate in your taste buds.

Wonderful Wine

Australia is ranked as the world's seventh-largest wine producer, and the finest Australian wines are among the best in the world - a judgment that is consistently confirmed at international wine shows.

Local Flavor

Visitors to Australia are often dazzled by the sheer quality and variety of Australia's food such as rock oysters and steak from outback. "Australians have one of the most extraordinary assortments of basic ingredients of high quality anywhere in the world" according to a leading US food writer, Barbara Kafka. The local food markets in every major city are a great place to sample the harvest.

Australian Cuisine

Australia's growing reputation as a heaven for foods is because of the mix of indigenous and multicultural influences. In any restaurant, the label 'Modern Australian Cuisine' is a promise that you'll be tantalized, delighted and surprised.

3.3 Shopping and Entertainment

Shopping is a part of any holiday, and a combination of fantastic shopping districts with exceptional style and all markets allow for hours of browsing or buying.

Shops are generally open from 9-5pm Monday through Friday (with the exception of Thursday when most stores will open until 9pm), 9-4pm on Saturday and some stores in the city will open on a Sunday but hours vary so it's best to call up and check.

You will find everything from traditional aboriginal items such as boomerangs, didgeridoos and bark paintings to contemporary arts and crafts. Original designs have been used to bring life to a wide variety of products, from home wares to clothing and jewelry.

Merino wool has a unique range of pure, itch-free, quality merino wool products, produced from Australian sheep carefully selected and bred for their soft handling wool.

Aboriginal art

Discussion Questions

1. Among the amazing experiences in Australia, which do you prefer to try?
2. What kind of products do travelers usually buy in Australia?
3. Have you ever tried Australian food? How's their taste?

Tips for Travelers

▣ Sydney Festival、 Every January, Australia's biggest city becomes even livelier.

As Australia's largest cultural event, Sydney Festival ensures Sydney is the place to stay during January. It is the celebration of summer and is synonymous with energy, style, spectacle, sophistication and world-class talent which so quintessentially define the city.

Sydney Festival

Australia
New Zealand
Canada
U.S.A.
Guam
Hawaii
the Northern Mariana Island

Chapter 2
New Zealand

Chapter 2 New Zealand

GETTING STARTED...

Location	Oceania, islands in the South Pacific Ocean, southeast of Australia
Climate	Temperate with sharp regional contrasts
Population	4,035,461
Ethnic group	European 69.8%, Maori 7.9%, Asian 5.7%, Pacific islander 4.4%, other 0.5%, mixed 7.8%, unspecified 3.8%
Religions	Anglican 14.9%, Roman Catholic 12.4%, Presbyterian 10.9%, Methodist 2.9%, Pentecostal 1.7%, Baptist 1.3%, other Christian 9.4%, other 3.3%, unspecified 17.2%, none 26%
Languages	English (official), Maori (official)

Scenery of New Zealand

Grammar Focus

1. A coordinate conjunction: and
A, B, C and D: A = B = C = D
diverse, sophisticated, <u>and</u> multicultural

2. Several meanings of conjunction: as
as = when　as = because　as well as = also
<u>As</u> they are believed to carry~.

3. Passive and active participle: -ed & - ing
Handcrafts <u>made</u> by local artists,
<u>Including</u> handmade jewelry~.

Vocabulary

landscape	diverse
sophisticate	steam
sweep	haven
relaxation	destination
occasion	acceptable
altitude	garment
specialty	carving
weaving	incorporate
replica	opportunity
abundance	pottery

UNIT 1 About New Zealand

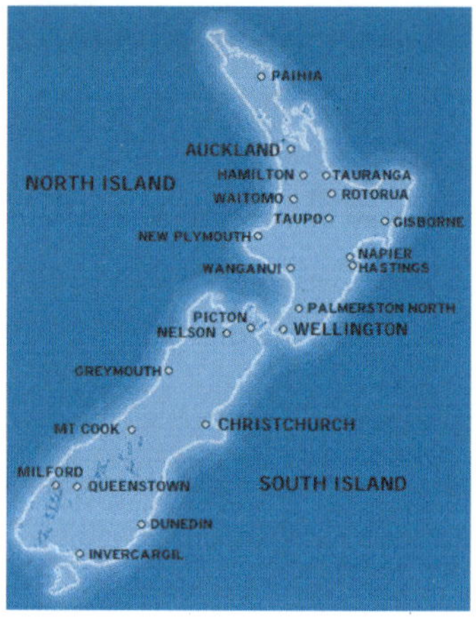

Map of New Zealand

New Zealand's awesome landscapes, lush forests, amazing wildlife and pleasant climate make it a heaven for many outdoor activities, and a great place to relax. The New Zealand society is diverse, sophisticated, and multicultural. The honesty, friendliness, and openness of New Zealander will impress you. The great advantage of New Zealand is that all of its diverse physical, cultural, and artistic landscapes are so close to each other.

New Zealand's spectacular landscape includes vast mountain chains, steaming volcanoes, sweeping coastlines, deeply indented fiords and lush rainforests. Comparable in size and shape to Great Britain, Colorado or Japan, New Zealand has a population of only 4 million - making it one of the world's least crowded countries. It is a haven for those seeking peace, and relaxation as well as a playground for thrill seekers and adventurers. A temperate climate with relatively small seasonal variation makes it an ideal year-round holiday destination.

The north of New Zealand is subtropical while the south is temperate. The warmest months are December, January and February, and the coldest June, July and August. In summer, the average maximum temperature ranges between 20-30℃ and in winter between 10-15℃.

Dress is informal and relaxed on most occasions. Smart casual clothes are acceptable at most restaurants and night-spots. Men are generally not expected to wear suits and ties, except in a few of the top formal bars and restaurants in major cities. In the summer, a light jacket or sweater should be included in your luggage because the weather turn cooler or you visit higher altitudes. You can expect some rain, so include a light rainproof jacket or coat. If you plan on visiting between May and September, pack warm winter clothes and layer your clothing.

New Zealand offers many different handmade arts and crafts, both European and Maori. Souvenir stores, museum shops, and specialty outlets often sell beautiful carvings, weaving and jewelry incorporating the ancient traditions and art forms of New Zealand's Maori people.

Ancient Maori crafts have become Taonga (precious treasures) to modern Maori. Traditional art heirlooms such as carved Rakau (walking sticks), Hei Taonga Pounamu (green stone or jade pendants) and bone carvings are treated with great respect and care, as they are believed to carry the spirit of their original owners and represent them to future generations.

It is possible to purchase replicas of artifacts to take back home, as well as recently made crafts in both traditional and modern designs. At the Maori Arts and Crafts Institute in Rotorua visitors have the opportunity to watch highly skilled Maori carvers and weavers at work.

New Zealand also has an abundance of European handcrafts made by local artists, including handmade jewelry, wooden and stuffed toys, hand knitted and crafted wool products, pottery etc.

Comprehension Check

1. New Zealand has a population of only 4 million - making it one of the world's (   ) crowded countries.

2. A temperate climate with relatively small seasonal variation makes it an ideal (   ) holiday destination.

3. The warmest months are (   ), January and February.

4. You can expect some (   ), so include a light rainproof jacket or coat.

5. New Zealand offers many different handmade arts and crafts; both (   ) and (   ).

6. (   ) are treated with great respect and care.

7. It is possible to purchase (   ) of artifacts to take back home.

8. New Zealand also has an abundance of (   ) handcrafts made by local artists.

Discussion Questions

1. Where is New Zealand?

2. Have you ever been to New Zealand?

3. Which part of New Zealand would you like to go?

4. If you had gone to New Zealand during the summer, what kind of clothing you should bring with?

5. Which season would you prefer to stay in New Zealand?

Useful Conversation

▣ When you are travel, you will face the situation in a flight.

A : Would you like to something to drink?

B : What kind of drink do you have?

A : Juice, beer, coke and wine something like that.

B : May I have a bottle of beer, please?

A : Yes, of course, and what would you like for dinner?

B : What is on the menu?

A : We have chicken and beef.

B : I'd like to have chicken, please.

A : Very well, sir.

B : Thank you very much.

Scenery of New Zealand

UNIT 2 Tourist Attractions

Grammar Focus

1. Expletive, there

There is a book.

There are books.

2. Have-possess

Have-auxiliary for perfect tense: have + pp

Visitors have the opportunity to experience…

New Zealand has had a colorful past.

Vocabulary

lift	panel
prepare	hemisphere
orbit	combination
original	scent
geothermal	urban
guarantee	relax
therapy	region
array	historic
spouting	geyser
crater	trout

2.1 Sky Tower, Auckland

Skyline of Auckland

Sky Tower is the tallest tower in the Southern hemisphere at 328 meters (1,000ft). With glass fronted lifts, glass floor panels, interactive technology and three public observation levels offering spectacular 360 degree views, Sky Tower is designed to take you to an all time high. Sky Tower also has a cafe - Sky Lounge and two restaurants; Orbit and the Observatory. Orbit is a revolving restaurant providing New Zealand cuisine. The Observatory is a unique combination of a luxurious style buffet restaurant. Also, located at the base of the Sky Tower is a gift shop. Sky Tower is part of skycity Auckland, one of New Zealand's leading entertainment destinations.

2.2 Rotorua

Rotorua is one of the original tourist destinations in New Zealand. It has been welcoming visitors for more than 200 years. From the moment people arrive in Rotorua they know they're somewhere quite different. At nearby geothermal hotspots, there are spouting geysers, boiling mud pools and warm geothermal springs. Silica terraces are naturally decorated with a variety of colors.

Rotorua is the heartland of New Zealand Maori culture, and visitors have the opportunity to experience the warm spirit of Maori. Although most of the Maori population lives in the urban areas, there are about 35 marae (meeting grounds) in the Rotorua district. You may be lucky to enough to stay as a guest on a marae because it gives you an unforgettable experience. Or you could catch a Maori cultural performance, where stories are relayed through beautiful song and dance. You can also enjoy in a traditional Hangi feast - the food is cooked below the ground in earthen ovens.

The Rotorua region is also one of New Zealand's prime trout fishing spots. You're practically guaranteed a catch, especially if a local professional guide is hired. Many of the volcanic crater lakes are home to a plentiful stock of trophy-sized rainbow trout.

Rotorua is quickly becoming known as Nature's Spa of the South Pacific. After a hard day's sightseeing or diverse activity, visitors can relax by soaking in the healing waters of the geothermal hot springs, or totally relax by choosing from a selection of therapeutic spa and massage therapies.

Geyser in Rotorua

2.3 Paradise in Queenstown

Scenes from all over the Queenstown Region were used in *The Lord of the Rings* movies. You can have a great time touring around linking them all together, while the adventure capital will offer an amazing array of activities to distract you along the way. An historic and well preserved gold mining village is about 20 minutes drive from Queenstown.

Closer to Queenstown, an exciting four-wheel drive (4WD) trip through Skippers Canyon will take you the spot used to portray the Fordlnad. Deer Park Heights, used for various locations in films, also affords great views. Travel through Queenstown to Glenorchy and you'll see why the locality of Paradise was so perfect for scenes in several international movies.

For an aerial perspective of the whole area, take a scenic "locations" flight, or, if you'd rather be closer to the ground, float on a raft down the river. You can even bungee jump into it.

Queenstown

2.4 Milford Sound

Milford Sound, described as the 'eighth wonder of the world', was carved out during successive ice ages and, at its deepest point off Miter Peak submerges to a depth of 265 meters. The grandeur of Milford Sound can be appreciated from the air or water. Bowen Falls, clashing 165 meters into the sea, and the Stirling Falls further down the Sound, set on the top of the towering cliffs and dwarfed by Miter Peak. It is truly spectacular after rain. Bottlenose dolphins, New Zealand fur seals and Fordland crested penguins are resident in the fiord and can be viewed up close from the cruises or kayak trips. A variety of cruises run daily on Milford Sound and overnight packages are also offered.

Milford Sound

Comprehension Check

1. Sky Tower is the (   ) tower in the Southern Hemisphere at 328 meters.
2. At nearby geothermal hotspots, there are spouting (   ), boiling mud pools and warm geothermal springs.
3. You can even (   ) into it in Queenstown.
4. Rotorua is quickly becoming known as (   ) of the South Pacific.
5. Milford Sound described as the 'eighth (   ) of the world', was carved out during successive ice ages.

Discussion Questions

1. Where would you prefer to stay in New Zealand?
2. What are the reasons people would like to visit Queenstown?
3. Do you enjoy seeing exotic animals such as fur seal and crested penguins?

Useful Conversation

▣ When you travel, you will have a chance to visit the bank.

A : Excuse me, where can I change some money?

B : Go to the first floor in this building.

A : Can I change Korean won to dollars?

B : Yes, you can.

A : What's the exchange rate today?

B : It's one thousand won to one dollar

A : I'd like to exchange one hundred thousand won.

B : Here's one hundred dollars. How would you like to have the money?

A : I'd like to have small money as much as possible.

B : Any other things that I can help you?

A : Sure, I'd like to have traveler's checks.

B : How much do you need?

A : I need one thousand dollars.

B : Please show your ID and signature.

A : Here they are.

B : Thanks, here's your traveler's check.

Lake of Wanaka, Queenstown

UNIT 3 Things to do

3.1 Amazing Experience

Jet Boat

Jet boating

Some of the most exciting jet boat trips are available near Queenstown and Canterbury.

Other areas include rivers in the South Island's Buller and Makarora regions; and in the North Island, on the Rangitaiki River, the Whanganui River and the Waikato River below the Huka Falls. Trips that combine jet boating with helicopter, and rafting or adventure tours are also popular.

Boat Cruise and Whale Watching

Relax on the deck and see New Zealand's beautiful coastline and waterways from a unique offshore perspective. You could find yourself cruising along glorious bays, island studded gulfs and sheltered waterways, or exploring inland rivers and lakes.

Dolphin Cruise

By boat you'll find magnificent scenery not visible from the roads as well as marine and bird life which may include penguins, seals or albatross. Sightseeing can be combined with activities like fishing, diving, and swimming with dolphins or even whale watching.

Rafting

With an enormous number of relatively short, fast-flowing rivers, New Zealand offers a range of rafting experiences that can be safely enjoyed by most adult visitors. Due to safety reasons, some operators may apply an age restriction of rafting.

New Zealand offers a variety of rafting options, with different excitement levels and trip lengths. Grade 1 rivers offer fairly calm waters, while grade 5 is regarded as extreme adventure. Trips range from a couple of hours to five days, and are led by qualified rafting guides who comply with established safety codes. All gear and special clothing is provided.

Rafting rivers in the North Island are mostly centered on the central East Coast areas of the Bay of Plenty (near Rotorua) and Hawke's Bay. In the South Island, the main areas are around the resort of Queenstown and on the West Coast.

Some operators offer a combined helicopter and rafting experience, and you can also try Black Water Rafting through underground caves.

Bungee jumping

The Bungee originates in New Zealand. Travelrs visit the home of the bungee jump, Queenstown. The historic Kawarau Bridge, 43 meters where the bungee phenomenon began, is the home to the new Kawarau Bungee Center featuring the Bungee Dome multi-media experience, and interactive and interpretive areas. There are the Ledge bungee, 47 meters with panoramic views of Q ueenstown, the Nevis High wire bungee, 134 meters, and New Zealand's highest and re-opening October 2004 the Pipeline Bungee in Skippers Canyon at 102 meters.

Kawarau bridge, Queenstown

3.2 Food and Dining

New Zealand's 'Pacific Rim' cuisine style takes its inspiration from regions and countries such as Europe, Thailand, Malaysia, Indonesia, Polynesia, Japan and Vietnam. This unique blend of influences has created a mouth-watering range of flavors and foods available from cafes and restaurants nationwide.

For dishes that have a distinctly New Zealand style look out for lamb and pork; salmon, crayfish, Bluff oysters, Paua (abalone), mussels and scallops; kumara (sweet potato); kiwifruit and tamarillo; and pavlova, the national dessert, made from meringue and lashings of fresh whipped cream topped with fresh fruit or berries.

While the main centers support a few elegant, silver-service restaurants, the trend is towards more relaxed cafe-bar dining. There is a wide variety of international food available including Japanese, Indian, Halal, Italian, Mexican, Chinese, Malaysian, and Thai. There are more than 900 Asian restaurants throughout New Zealand.

Shopping and Entertainment

Most shops and businesses are open from 9am to 5pm, Monday to Friday. Many stores are also open on Saturdays and some are open on Sundays. In resorts you will find most stores open in the evenings. Banks are closed on weekends.

New Zealand offers a huge variety of shopping from arts and craft markets, galleries and museum shops to exclusive designer stores. For traditional New Zealand souvenirs look for examples of superb Maori carvings in wood, bone and pounamu (green stone or jade). You can also find jewelry and ornaments made from the paua shell (abalone), treasured by Maori for centuries.

New Zealand potters are recognized as among the world's finest today. Many fine artisans also work with stone, wood, glass and metals. The country's vast wool industry makes it possible to find wonderful hand knitted wool sweaters, beautiful wall hangings, homespun yarns and top-quality sheepskins.

Alongside top international fashion in boutique stores in the main city areas, you will also find New Zealand's own award winning fashion labels, including Zambesi, Nomd, and Karen Walker.

Street market, Queenstown

Discussion Questions

1. What type of activities would you like to do in New Zealand?
2. Have you ever tried any adventurous sports?
3. Have you ever tried bungee jumping?
4. Do you mind having an original New Zealand cuisine? If so, what do you prefer to have?
5. If you can bring only one thing from New Zealand, what will it be?

Tips for travelers

▣ New Zealand International Arts Festival, February-March Wellington, New Zealand

New Zealand's biggest and best international festival for all the arts - music, theater, opera, dance, writers, readers, etc. Features many top acts from around the globe.

B&B in New Zealand

English & Culture in Tourism

Australia
New Zealand
Canada
U.S.A
Guam
Hawaii
the Northern Mariana Island

Chapter 3
Canada

Chapter 3

Canada

GETTING STARTED...

Location Northern North America, bordering the North Atlantic Ocean on the east, North Pacific Ocean on the west, and the Arctic Ocean on the north, north of the US.

Climate Varies from temperate in south to sub arctic and arctic in north

Population 32,805,041

Ethnic groups British Isles origin 28%, French origin 23%, other European 15%, Amerindian 2%, other, mostly Asian, African, Arab 6%, mixed background 26%

Religions Roman Catholic 42.6%, Protestant 23.3% (including United Church 9.5%, Anglican 6.8%, Baptist 2.4%, Lutheran 2%), other Christian 4.4%, Muslim 1.9%, other and unspecified 11.8%, none 16%

Languages English (official) 59.3%, French (official) 23.2%, other 17.5%

Vancouver, British Columbia

Grammar Focus

1. Tense

Past perfect, Past, present, future

had + pp, -ed, -, will be

The Vikings had tried to settle in northern New Foundland.

Columbus discovered America in 1492.

English and French are the country's official languages.

You will probably have to fly.

2. The comparative degree

more than

much more interesting than flying

Vocabulary

bounty	official
prehistoric	tribe
aboriginal	religious
craft	distinct
prairies	average
temperature	shivering
festival	attraction
distance	extensive
transportation	strap
operate	

UNIT 1 About Canada

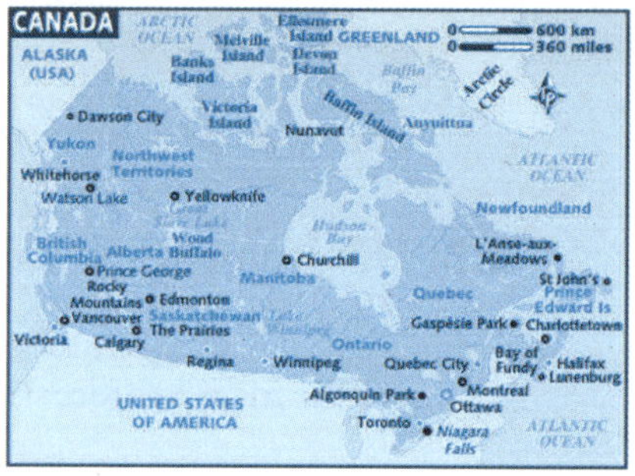

Map of Canada

The second largest country in the world has sights enough to keep you going for several lifetimes. Its wild bounty of nature parks hold bald eagles, bears, lynxes, wolves and thousand year old pines. English and French are the country's official languages, though the province of New Brunswick is the only officially bilingual area in the country.

Canada has four distinct seasons, although their arrival times vary across the country. The single most significant factor in climate is latitude. As a rule of thumb, it gets colder the further north you go, so it's no accident that the warmest areas in the south are the most populated. The western and eastern coasts are both very wet, though much of the rain falls during winter. In Saskatchewan, Manitoba and eastern Alberta the prairies are fairly dry all year. Canadian winters are long and hard: in more than two-thirds of the country, the average January temperature is a shivering -18°C (-0.4°F). July and August are the warmest months, when temperatures in the south are usually in the upper 20°Cs (low 80°Fs).

Spring, summer and autumn are all ideal for touring, though if you want to ski you'll naturally have to come in winter or early spring. For campers and those who want to visit the far north, the summer months of July and August are best. Summer is also when many of the country's festivals take place. Note that the peak tourist season is between Victoria Day (late May) and Labor Day (early September). Although spring and autumn have fewer crowds, lower prices and a more relaxed pace than the summer months, some visitor-oriented facilities and attractions may be closed during these shoulder seasons.

Granvill Island, Vancouver

Land travel is much cheaper and, if you don't mind long distances, much more interesting than flying. The bus network is the most extensive public transportation system and is generally less expensive than the limited train service. The country's most famous train is the Canadian, a classic 1950s-style beauty that travels from Toronto to Vancouver (Canada's longest continuous train route), complete with a two-storied windowed 'dome car' for sightseeing.

Air fares are fairly expensive but, if you're strapped for time, the distances you may need to travel are so great that you'll probably have to fly. Air Canada is the major domestic airline. In many ways, the best way to experience the country is to hire a car. Canadians drive on the right side of the road, as in the US. A valid driver's license from any country is good in Canada for three months.

Comprehension Check

1. The ( )-largest country in the world has sights enough to keep you going for several lifetimes.
2. ( ) and ( ) are the country's two official languages.
3. Canada has ( ) distinct seasons, although their arrival times vary across the country.
4. Land travel is much ( ) and, if you don't mind long distances, much more interesting than flying.
5. The country's most famous train is the ( ), a classic 1950s-style beauty that travels from Toronto to Vancouver.

Discussion Questions

1. Have you ever been to Canada?
2. What have you known about Canada?
3. Does Canada have two official languages? How about your country?
4. If you traveled to Canada, which transportation would you take a car, train, or flight?
5. Which part of Canada would you prefer to travel?

Useful Conversation

▣ When you travel, you need to rent a car.

A : I'd like to rent a car.

B : Yes, sir, what kind of cars would you like?

A : I'd like to see a list of your rate.

B : Here it is.

A : I want to rent this car for a week. Do I pay in advance?

B : Yes, you do. May I see your drivers' license?

A : Here you are.

B : Do you want to be insured?

A : Yes, I want liability insurance. Please show me a list of your rates.

B : Here it is.

A : Thank you very much.

Victoria, British Columbia

UNIT 2 Tourist Attractions

Grammar Focus

1. as adjective as

as large as, as good as, as much as

2. Passive sentence

S + be + pp

It was saved by the foresight of the city father.

3. Active sentence

S + be + ing

It was playing Jazz music.

Vocabulary

asset	peninsula
foresight	preserve
facility	counterclockwise
frequent	tide
totem poles	residential
estate	veritable
wander	canopy
emphasis	accompaniment
rejuvenating	escape
inspiration	encompassing

2.1 British Columbia

Stanley Park

The 1,000 acre Stanley Park, which covers an area as large as Vancouver of downtown, is a wonderful asset for a city already bountifully blessed with natural landscape. Mostly forested, the park extends to the very tip of the peninsula at the Narrows, the entrance to Burrard Inlet.

Stanley Park, Vancouver

The peninsula was a military zone that would have no doubt been clear cut, but it was saved by the foresight of the city fathers, who claimed to preserve it within Vancouver founding in 1886. Facilities and attractions are abundant, but the main function of Stanley Park is the vast open space, directly accessible from the city, where people can walk, rollerblade, cycle, swim, or just relax. A ride along the 6-mile scenic road that runs one way counterclockwise around the shore is an essential experience for all visitors, best undertaken by rented bicycles with frequent stops to savor the ever changing views of city, sea, and mountain.

As the road curves around Coal Harbor with its Royal Yacht Club and Rowing Club, bird-rich Lost Lagoon is to the left, a former inlet that almost dries up at low tide. Among the trees just short of Hallelujah Point is a brightly painted group of totem poles. Near Prospect Point, the path crosses over the approach to the 5,000 foot long [1,524-meter long] Lions Gate Bridge, built in 1938 to link the city with the exclusive residential area of West Vancouver.

There is a fine view of ships passing in and out of Burrard Inlet from Prospect Point. Between here and the west-facing Ferguson Point, the forest of cedar, hemlock, and Douglas fir gives a good idea of what the site of Vancouver must have looked like before clearance began in the 1880s.

Butchart Gardens, Victoria

Located on Vancouver Island, the Butchart Gardens began as the turn of the century effort to beautify a quarry site on the estate of Mr. and Mrs. R P Butchart. Since its inception, Butchart Gardens has grown into a veritable Eden, covering fifty acres with all the colors of nature. Butchart Gardens is a place where life still runs at the pace of a bygone era, and the gracious traditions of the past live on.

Butchart Garden, Victoria

Spring lives on throughout the winter at the Butchart inside a huge conservatory. While the snow falls outside, you can wander under a canopy of spring flowers as koi and goldfish splash in a sapphire stream. During the spring and summer, the emphasis shifts to the outdoors. Live entertainment, light shows and fireworks highlight the evenings. The live music that fills the air every afternoon makes a perfect accompaniment to a refined meal at any one of the Gardens' restaurants. A trip to Butchart Gardens is a unique, sun-dappled escape that will leave you bursting with fresh inspiration.

Banff National Park

Lake Louise, Banff

The origins of the first Canadian national parks go back to 1883, when railway builders came across hot springs, which are called Banff Hot Springs Reserve. The park would burble outward to its present size by 1902, and it is encompassing cloud-veiled peaks, vast glaciers, raucous rivers, unbelievably blue-green lakes, and magnificent hotels. Today the park has four million visitors annually arriving mainly via road network that puts them at easy reach of hiking, biking, boating, skiing, and almost any other recreational activities.

2.2 Ontario

CN Tower, Toronto

CN Tower, the unmistakable urban icon, shoots an extraordinary 1,815 feet into the air, a fluted concrete column contrasting with the Sky Dome crouching nearby. It is still the tallest freestanding structure in the world, high enough for the Sky pod and the top like spike to pierce low cloud cover, or for visitors to look down on aircraft heading for the city in the international airport.

The tower was built in 1976, not only as a telecommunications facility but as the centerpiece for a vast urban redevelopment project that never took place. In any event, it has more than earned its keep as a visitor attraction.

The view is the thing, of course, both from the observation decks of the Sky pod (1,136 feet) and the even higher Space Deck. On the ride up the outside elevator, there is the additional challenge of the glass floor, with only space between your feet and the Sky Dome in field far below. There is a revolving restaurant, and, at the base of the tower, more thrills such as laser games.

Niagara Falls

Niagara Fall, Ontario

The city of Niagara Falls, known to many as the "honeymoon capital of the world," is home to one of the greatest natural wonders in the world. An astounding 150 million liters of thundering white water tumble over Niagara Falls every minute, and the mist from falls makes in massive clouds that blanket the city. The falls sound forbidden, but they're actually quite accessible.

Visitors can slip on raingear and board the Maid of the Mist to navigate the tempest at the base of the falls. You can get above it all in a cable car ride over the rapids and whirlpools. Or board a helicopter and take to the skies for an unforgettable view. If you prefer to stay on the land, the Skylon and Minolta towers standing above Niagara Falls offer an 80-mile view of the surrounding region. The entire area is a tourist Mecca, and the falls themselves are only the beginning of the fun.

2.3 Quebec

Quebec City

Quebec is home to some of the earliest outposts and settlements in North America, and the Québecois culture is every bit as vibrant and distinct as it was centuries ago. No surprise, then, that Québec's museums and galleries are popular destinations for visitors from around the world.

The Canadian Museum of Civilization in Gatineau (just across the river from the nation's capital, Ottawa), traces 1,000 years of settlement in Canada, and also houses a stunning IMAX/Omni max theater in an impressively designed building that pays homage to Canada's first nations people.

City hall, Quebec

The Montréal Museum of Fine Arts, which is over 140 years old, was Canada's first art museum, and its collection of everything from paintings to furniture is not to be missed. Close by, the Canadian Center for Architecture focuses on the evolution of cityscapes and the manmade environment. Don't miss its stunning sculpture garden.

Iin towns and cities across the province, you will discover unique "economic-museums" highlighting local history and demonstrations of regional arts and crafts, from stained glass to bookbinding to whiskey making. Let your feet take you where they will; no matter where you go, it will be a voyage of discovery.

Montreal, Quebec

Montreal, in the province of Quebec, is a bilingual metropolis that has cultural part of both North American and European. Montreal's charm lies in its relaxed atmosphere rather than its star attractions. Nonetheless, this city of immigrants has managed to carve out a place for itself as Quebec's economic and cultural center. It's also friendly and easy to get around.

Quebec's largest city, Montreal, has always kept one foot in the countryside, although mighty skyscrapers have sprung up among the city's churches. During the day, the city has a typically North American bustle, though French-speaking Montreal takes pains to retain its linguistic heritage.

Night view of Montreal

Comprehension Check

1. The 1,000-acre (   ) is a wonderful asset for a city already bountifully blessed with natural landscape.

2. Today Banff National park has annual (   ) visitors arrive mainly via a road network.

3. The CN Tower is still the (   ) freestanding structure in the world.

4. Visitors can slip on (   ) and board the Maid of the Mist to navigate the tempest at the base of the falls.

5. The (   ) of Fine Arts, which is over 140 years old, was Canada's first art museum.

6. Montreal, in the province of Quebec, is a (   ) metropolis that has culturally part North American and part European.

Discussion Questions

1. How big is Stanley Park in Vancouver?

2. When you travel to Canada, would you stay in Banff or Toronto?

3. What is the tallest freestanding structure in the world? Do you know what the next tallest one is?

4. Which place is popular for honeymooners? What factors attract them?

Useful Conversation

■ When you travel, you can't stay without food.

A : We need a table for two, please.
B : Yes, sir, come this way, here's your table.
A : Thank you.
B : May I take your order now?
A : Can I have a menu, please?
B : Yes, sir, here it is.
A : I'll take fillet mignon.
B : Very well, sir, how would you like your fillet mignon, sir?
A : Medium well-done, please.
B : What would you like to order, sir?
C : Would you recommend a specialty of the house?
B : Yes, how about Bulgogi?
C : What's Bulgogi?
B : It's barbecued beef, prepared Korean style, sir. The most popular Korean dish among foreigners must be Bulgogi. Marinated beef sliced grilled over charcoal will remind you of American barbecue.
C : Do you serve it with rice?
B : Yes, sir. We also serve Kimchi with it.
C : Very nice. I'd like to have it.
B : What would you like to drink?
A : A glass of wine, please.
C : Please, bring me a bottle of beer.
B : What kind of dessert would you like, sir?
A : Two chocolate cake, please.
B : Thank you very much.

UNIT 3 Things to do

3.1. Amazing Experience

Dog-sledding

Ski in Canada

Dog-sledding is truly a Canadian activity. You will be thrilled on this traditional mode of transportation as you lead your own dog team along trails through primitive valleys and mountain ridges. You can look for dog-sledding adventures in British Columbia, Alberta, Saskatchewan, Quebec, Ontario, Yukon, Nunavut and Northwest Territories. Dog-sledding trips will vary with the location, but can be several days or longer. The dog-sledding season runs from December to April.

Ski in Rocky

Artic Cruise from Greenland to Banff Island

Canada's downhill ski resorts are second to none in the world. Whether it's skiing in the Alberta Rocky Mountains, the Coastal range in British Columbia, or the fantastic rugged interior mountains, there is a mountain to match your downhill skiing ability. Lodges and resorts offer deluxe accommodations in many areas.

Artic cruise

Artic Cruise

Explore the culture and history of the north on this high arctic cruise to Canada and Greenland. On this journey, you will explore one of the worlds' largest bird cliffs at Apparsuit where thousands of guillemots, northern divers and somber cormorants breed. You will sail through Illuissat, where the icebergs, some over 300 feet high, lumber down this famous fiord and you will visit the scared graves of the ill-fated Franklin Expedition on lonely Beechy Island. You will also have a chance to interact with local Inuit communities, learning about their culture and history.

Wildlife watching safari

Artic wolf

You can view the arctic wildlife, which consists of arctic wolves, caribou and musk-ox. There are few places left on earth that are unaltered by man; one such place is the barren lands in the Northwest Territories. Situated in the vast Precambrian Shield, this unique landscape of bedrock glaciated hills covered in lichen, wild flowers and shrubs is a magnet for large populations of tundra wildlife. You will travel near the Thelon Game Sanctuary, the largest and most remote wildlife refuge in the world.

3.2. Food and Dining

European style restaurant

Travelers do not need to go to Europe to have a culinary vacation. Victoria and Vancouver Island have it all - fresh seafood, pasture raised meats, artisan cheeses, outstanding organic produce and wild foods from the forest.

Local chefs and residents alike support the farmers on the Saanich Peninsula and in the Cowichan Valley who produce such high quality foods. Visitors can experience the Island's bounty in many of Victoria's restaurants, but local markets or a Gourmet Farm and Winery Tour are also entertaining ways to get a taste of Victoria.

During the summer, markets are held throughout the city where local farmers sell their produce and local artisans sell their wares. Visitors can literally spend an entire weekend "market-hopping" while taking in the spectacular scenery of Vancouver Island. Visitors can also buy fresh produce from the farm gate or from the roadside stands that are scattered all over the country roads.

3.3 Shopping and Entertainment

Shopping in British Columbia

Once referred to as Vancouver's Little Italy and now called simply "The Drive," Commercial Drive is one of the most cosmopolitan areas in North America. It's a bohemian community, where you'll encounter writers, painters, poets and musicians, where you'll discover great bargains on everything from radical literature, organic tofu and hemp products to retro furniture, classic clothing and vintage vinyl, and where dedicated shoppers will feel right at home. The city is also home to fashion hotspots like Robson Street, Gas town and Yale town, where brand names give way to designer labels, and some of the country's most exciting fashioners make their homes.

In Victoria, the Market Square is the place to browse for such west coast delicacies as smoked salmon or pick up aboriginal artifacts like handmade jewelry, ceremonial masks and carvings meticulously crafted from island cedar. Visit Government Street (Victoria's version of L.A.'s Rodeo Drive) for quirky gifts, vintage and designer clothing, and furniture and a box of Cuban cigars. Not far away, you'll find Victoria's Chinatown (the oldest in Canada), where you can explore a maze of bustling, crowded shops.

Public market, Vancouver

Leaving the cities behind, you can pick up souvenirs at an Okanagan winery or one of the region's many wine festivals. The farmers' markets in Prince George and at Lonsdale Quay and Granville Island offer fresh produce and crafts, and have become Mecca for people from all walks of life. When you've worked up an appetite from a day of shopping, any one of British Columbia farmers' markets is a perfect place to make pleasure of your taste for fresh gourmet food. The province also boasts a number of large shopping centers that range from high-fashion to bargain basement.

Shopping in Ontario

If you plan on visiting Ontario, make sure to leave some space in your suitcase for souvenirs. The province is home to some of the best shopping in Canada, and with a great exchange rate (every American dollar is worth about 30% more here), there's no reason not to give in to your shopaholic tendencies.

There's no better place to shop for Canadian than in the nation's capital, Ottawa. Within sight of Parliament Hill, you'll find the Byward Market, which hosts a local farmer's market in the summer and fall and is a year round home to high-fashion boutiques, galleries, cafés and nightclubs. Nearby, the Rideau Center houses hundreds of stores are in an elegant setting. And Sparks Street, just south of Parliament Hill, is the perfect place to shop for a souvenir. Don't miss the chance to taste a bottle of real Canadian maple syrup.

Sample the bounty of Ontario's wineries on the Niagara Peninsula or Pelee Island and pick up a bottle of Ontario ice wine, a delicacy known locally as "liquid gold". And throughout the province, you'll discover small towns where antique stores and folk art galleries capture the charm of Ontario's rural lifestyle.

Thousand island, Toronto

Discussion Questions

1. Have ever tried or seen dog-sledding? If so, where?
2. What types of activities would you prefer to try in Canada?
3. When you are in Canada, are you going to shop in downtown? Which area would you prefer to shop?
4. What is the specialty of Canada?
5. When you think of the country, Canada, what comes to mind?

Tips for Travelers

▣ Toronto International Film Festival

Two major events in Toronto are Caribbean, held in August, which is a cultural exchange offering ethnic music, dance and food, and the Gay Pride Day Parade through the downtown area, which takes place in June. In September, there's the Toronto International Film Festival. Calgary hosts the popular Calgary Stampede in July, the highlight of which is the chuck wagon race and rodeo. In the west, Victoria celebrates the First Peoples' Festival in August with traditional craftwork, dancing and war-canoe rides.

▣ Events Calendar

Some public holidays are only celebrated regionally. They are: 3rd Monday in February - Family Day (Alberta); Monday nearest March 17 - St Patrick's Day (Newfoundland); Monday nearest April 23 - St George's Day (Newfoundland); June 24 - National Day (or St-Jean-Baptists Day, Québec); Monday nearest June 24 - Discovery Day (Newfoundland); Monday nearest July 12 - Orangemen's Day (Newfoundland), and 3rd Monday in August - Discovery Day (Yukon).

Chapter 4
United States of America

Australia
New Zealand
Canada
U.S.A.
Guam
Hawaii
the Northern Mariana Island

Chapter 4

United States of America

GETTING STARTED...

Climate	Mostly temperate, but tropical in Hawaii and Florida, arctic in Alaska, semiarid in the great plains west of the Mississippi River, and arid in the Great Basin of the southwest
Population	295,734,134
Ethnic groups	White 81.7%, black 12.9%, Asian 4.2%, Amerindian and Alaska native 1%, native Hawaiian and other Pacific islander 0.2%
Religions	Protestant 52%, Roman Catholic 24%, Mormon 2%, Jewish 1%, Muslim 1%, other 10%, none 10%
Languages	English 82.1%, Spanish 10.7%, other Indo-European 3.8%, Asian and Pacific island 2.7%, other 0.7%

Manhattan, NY

Grammar focus

1. Relative Pronoun: who, whose, whom

Migrants whose primary goal was to colonize.

I like a man who is handsome.

I like a man whom my friend loves.

2. Noun + of + noun

a parade of explores

a friend of mine

Vocabulary

landscape	regionalism
mythology	incredibly
population	Declaration of Independence
temperate	extreme
continent	inhabitant
descendant	pageantry
odd	glam
terrorism	imperative
immigration	seaport
require	digital

UNIT 1 About the US

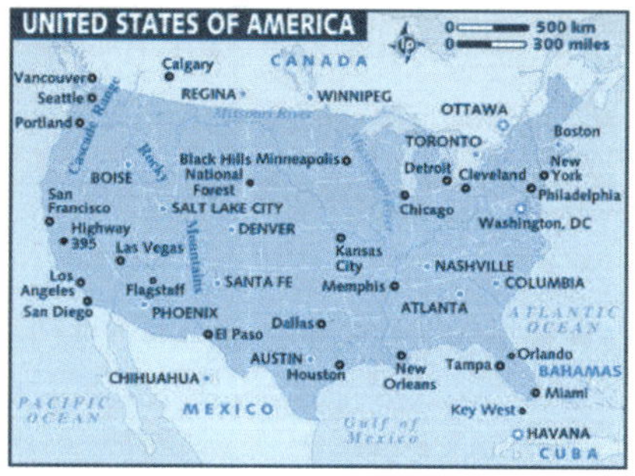

Map of United States of America

The US is home to several of the world's most exciting cities, some truly mind blowing landscapes, a strong sense of regionalism, mythology, more history than the country gives itself credit for and, arguably, some of the most approachable natives in the world.

The US was fashioned from an incredibly various population who, with little in common apart from a desire to choose their own paths to wealth or heaven, rallied around the ideals of the Declaration of Independence to forge the richest, most inventive and most powerful country on earth.

The climate is temperate in most of the US. Generally, it gets hotter the further south you go and seasonally more extreme the further you are north and inland from the coasts. Winters in the northeast and upper Midwest can bring long periods below freezing even though it's still warm enough to swim at the beaches in Florida and Southern California.

It's believed that the continent's first inhabitants walked into North America across what is now the Bering Strait from Asia. For the next 20,000 years these pioneering settlers were essentially left alone to develop distinct and dynamic cultures.

In the modern US, their descendants include the Pueblo people in what is now New Mexico; Apache in Texas; Navajo in Arizona, Colorado and Utah; Hopi in Arizona; Crow in Montana; Cherokee in North Carolina; and Mohawk and Iroquois in New York State.

Americans love parades and pageantry, so there's no shortage of events and festivals. Half the country comes to a standstill during the Super Bowl, the American football championship held in late January. New Orleans' Mardi Gras, in February or March, is a rowdy, touristy. St Patrick's Day, in mid-March, is celebrated with parades and pitchers of green beer; it's especially fervent in New York and Chicago. The Kentucky Derby is raced in Louisville in May.

Independence Day (the Fourth of July) is celebrated with lots of flag-waving patriotism, fireworks and the odd beverage. Travelers should drop into the National Hobo Convention in Britt, Iowa, in August. Halloween (October 31) is a big deal for kids, who go trick-or-treating around their neighborhood; in Greenwich Village, West Hollywood and San Francisco the holiday is celebrated with glam parades. Americans go home for a big feed on Thanksgiving, the fourth Thursday of November.

The Your main option for getting to the US is either by air or, from the closer countries, by road or train. The main international airports are in Boston, New York, Washington, Miami, Chicago, Dallas-Fort Worth, Houston, Atlanta, Denver, Seattle, San Francisco and Los Angeles, with hundreds of smaller airports dotted all over the country. For those traveling into the US from Canada or Mexico, you have the option of driving, catching a bus or an Amtrak train.

The US is regularly adjusting entry requirements in efforts to reduce the threat of terrorism. It is imperative that travelers double- and triple-check current regulations before coming to the US, as changes will occur for several years. A procedure introduced in 2004 requires most visitors traveling on visas to the United States to have two fingerprints scanned by an inkless device and a digital photograph taken by immigration officials upon entry at US air and seaports.

Comprehension Check

1. The US was fashioned from an incredibly (   ) population.
2. The climate is (   ) in most of the US.
3. It's believed that the continent's first inhabitants walked into North America across what is now the (   ) from Asia.
4. Americans love (   ) and pageantry, so there's no shortage of events and festivities.
5. Your main option for getting to the US is either by (   ) or, from the closer countries, by road or (   ).
6. (   ) in the European tradition do not exist in the United States.

Discussion Questions

1. Have you ever been to the United States?
2. Is entering the US difficult for tourist? If so, what are the requirements to enter?
3. Are there any misconceptions that we've known about the US? If so, what are they?

Useful Conversation

▣ When you travel, you will ask a question where the tourist attraction is on a street.

A : Can you tell me how to get to Gugenheim museum?

B : Yes, go straight on 5th avenue, and turn right onto 58th street. Walk three blocks to Museum avenue. You will see Gugenheim on your right.

A : I'm sorry, but I don't get it. Could you say that again, please?

B : Ok, first you go straight, and turn right onto 58th street. Do you follow me?

A : Yes, I follow you now.

B : Then you walk down three blocks more.

A : Yes.

B : There's Gugenheim on your right side. You can't miss it.

A : Now, I've got it. Thank you very much.

B : No, it's my pleasure.

UNIT 2 Tourist Attractions

Grammar Focus

1. Apposition

-rename or explain of noun.

Beverly Hills, home of the movie stars, is ~.

2. Preposition + noun (or-ing)

in the entire world, without seeing

3. is worth - ing

It is worth seeing ~.

Vocabulary

splendid	architecture
replicas	flamboyant
amusement	metropolitan
vibrant	myriad
volcanic	tropical
retreat	subtropical
alpine	pastoral
ascend	mesa
precipitous	grove
arctic	capital

2.1 Western States

Las Vegas, Nevada

Las Vegas is the largest center for adult entertainment in the entire world. It offers gambling, splendid entertainment and unbelievably expensive architecture. Giant pyramids of glass, multicolored fantasy castles, replicas of the Eiffel Tower and the New York skyline rise out of the Nevada desert. Even if you don't gamble or party, it is worth seeing this flamboyant display. In addition, Las Vegas is conveniently located near some of the greatest natural scenery in the southwest including the Grand Canyon Zion and Death Valley. It is only a half-day drive from Los Angeles.

Skyline of Las Vegas

Yosemite National Park, California

Yosemite National Park contains one of the most beautiful alpine valleys ever seen. 2,000 feet high vertical granite cliffs with nearly a dozen cascading waterfalls surround the glacially eroded Yosemite Valley.

Outside the popular valley, this immense park contains groves of giant Sequoia trees, alpine meadows

Yosemite National Park, California

and snow-capped peaks. It is a paradise for rock climbers, backpackers, campers, photographers and tourists.

Los Angeles, California

Hollywood Sign, L.A.

Los Angles is the second largest city in the US and the largest metropolitan center on the west coast. It includes many different communities including Hollywood, home of the movie makers, and Beverly Hills, home of the movie stars. L.A. has a pleasant subtropical climate with many miles of white sand beaches and the famous "California Surf." It is conveniently located near many scenic attractions like the spectacular coastline of Big Surf, the alpine wilderness of the Sierra Nevada Mountains and the simple beauty of the Mojave Desert. It is only a half-day drive to Las Vegas, Nevada.

San Francisco, California

San Francisco is the other great city in California. It is smaller than Los Angeles and does not have the warm tropical beaches, but it is much more scenic. Hillside streets lined with Victorian houses overlook a large blue bay surrounded by pastoral mountains. Historic cable cars still ascend the steep streets, and the magnificent Golden Gate Bridge frames its Pacific inlet. The nearby Marin headlands and Muir woods provide scenic diversions. It is less than an hour drive to the Napa Valley and Sonoma Valley wine country, and a half-day to beautiful Yosemite National Park.

Golden Gate Bridge

2.2 Central States

The Grand Canyon National Park, Arizona

The Grand Canyon National Park in Arizona is one of the greatest natural wonders of the world. It is a mile deep (1,500 meters) and over 15 miles (20 km) wide by 100 miles (150 km) long. The interior of the Canyon is adorned with a vast maze of multicolored mesas, cliffs and headlands punctuated by a maze of smaller canyons and valleys. The ever-changing play of sun and shadow on the multihued

Grand Canyon

rock layers produces a breathtaking display which is the best scene from the visitor's center on the south rim. The only access to the interior of the canyon is by hiking or by riding mules down the precipitous trails.

New Orleans, Louisia

Parade on Mardi Gras

New Orleans is the most European flavored city in the US. Spanish and French cultures blended with Afro-American and Caribbean influences form this exotic city at the mouth of the Mississippi River. New Orleans is famous for Jazz music, wild nightlife and its fine Cajun cuisine. Every February, the entire city goes mad for a week long carnival celebration known as Mardi Gras. Tourists flock to New Orleans all year round to sample the great food and to enjoy the nightlife.

2.3 Eastern States

New York City, New York

Time Square, New York City

New York City is the largest metropolitan center in the US. It is famous for the Statue of Liberty, Empire State building, United Nations, museums, Broadway theaters, restaurants, Times Square, nightlife and shopping. It is a huge vibrant city that never seems to sleep. There are many opportunities for entertainment in its myriad of nightclubs, bars, theaters, and sports arenas. There are lots of cultural attractions in its museums, art galleries and concert halls.

Washington DC

White House

Washington DC, the capital of the US, is a beautiful and interesting city. It is filled with numerous monuments, museums and public parks including the White House, the US Capital and many other government buildings. There are plenty of interesting things to see in Washington, and most of them are completely free. Washington has a diverse population and a great variety of ethnic restaurants. It is only an hour drive to the port city of Baltimore and a half-day drive to New York City.

Orlando, Florida

Disney land, Orlando

Orlando is the largest center for family entertainment in the entire world. It offers Disney World, the largest family amusement complex on this planet, plus Universal Studios, Sea World, Wet and Wild and several other major attractions. Hundreds of smaller amusement and entertainments are located nearby. You can spend weeks in Orlando without seeing it all. In addition, Florida offers wonderful tropical beaches and year-round golf and tennis.

Comprehension Check

1. Giant pyramids of glass, multicolored fantasy castles, (   ) of the Eiffel Tower and the New York skyline rise out of the Nevada desert.

2. Orlando offers (   ), the largest family amusement complex on this planet.

3. (   ) is famous for the Statue of Liberty, Empire State building, United Nations, museums, Broadway theaters, restaurants, Times Square, nightlife and shopping.

4. (   ) is a mile deep 1,500meters and over 15miles(20 km) wide by 100 miles (150 km) long.

5. Washington DC, the (   ) of the US, is a beautiful and interesting city.

Discussion Questions

1. Which attractions would you like to explore?

2. What makes New York City so famous for people?

3. How would people access the interior of the Grand Canyon?

4. When is the best time to visit New Orleans?

Useful Conversation

▣ When you travel, the shopping center is not a place that you can miss it.

A : May I help you, sir?

B : I'd like to get a sweater like this, but I can't find one in my size.

A : What size of sweater do you wear?

B : I wear size 4

A : Let me see, I'm sorry, we don't have that size here

B : That's all right. Could you show me another?

A : Sure, how about this one?

B : Where can I try it on?

A : The dressing room is over there, on the corner of the desk.

B : Thanks.

A : Do you like it?

B : Oh, it fits well. I'd like to buy it.

UNIT 3 Things to do

3.1 Amazing Experiences

There are still places in the US where you can drive for many miles and see no trace of civilization. In the Sierra Nevada Mountains and the Rocky Mountains, you can rent horses and pack mules and ride for days in unspoiled wilderness without seeing another person. Nearly every state offers a wide choice of hiking trails, backpacking areas and campgrounds. Some states offer unique wilderness experiences.

San Francisco Bay Cruise

Driving map of Western California

This loop drive begins in many travelers. Favorite American city, San Francisco, which you will explore from the top of Telegraph Hill to the bottom of the chowder bowls on Fisherman's Wharf, is situated on the tip of a peninsula, upon which the route leads south to San Jose, the capital of Silicon Valley. Then you return north along the east side of San Francisco Bay, passing through small historic towns and the university city of Berkeley before arriving back in San Francisco. There is a city that has it all great-swelling views, a picturesque bay that is by turns sunny or shrouded in romantic fog, Victorian houses on steep hills, fine restaurants, and high culture.

Taking a photo with Mickey Mouse

Mickey mouse in Disney Land

From the charm of Main Street to the whimsy of Mickey's Toontown, visitors explore eight fantastic "lands" of nostalgia, color and delight in Disney Land. A must see at Disney lands park is Indian Jones adventure, Mickey's house and meeting Mickey, virtual reality games, multimedia experiences, exciting show, and Walt Disney's parade that make your dreams come true. Don't miss taking photo with Mickey and his friends whom you can meet anywhere in Disney Land.

Gamble on the fortune

Coca Cola museum in Las Vagas

Las Vegas, an ever-changing fantasy-land of a city, has seen unbelievable expansion since it emerged from the desert 100 years ago. Thirty-seven million visitors enjoy the sights and sounds of Las Vegas every year. Travelers stay in some of the most glamorous, unique hotels in the world. They eat at five-star restaurants and expansive buffets. They play at casinos, pools, health spas and golf courses. Sometimes (many times, actually) they even marry each other.

Exploring Hoover Dam & Lake Meadow

Exploring Hoover Dam & Lake Meadow

The Hoover Dam is a testimony to a country's ability to construct monolithic projects in the midst of adverse conditions. Built during the Depression; thousands of men and their families came to Black Canyon to tame the Colorado River. It took less than 5 years, in a harsh and barren land, to build the largest dam of its time. You can't miss the grandeur size of artificial view during the exploration.

Camping in Grand Canyon National Park

South Rim of Grand Canyon

This canyon is a gift what people can experience. Its timelessness provokes a comparison to our short existence. In its vast spaces we may find comfort from our hectic lives. The Grand Canyon we visit today is a gift from past generations. Grand Canyon is heavily visited for most of the year and it is imperative to plan ahead for lodging, camping, or mule trips. Persons planning day visits only should arrive early in the day as parking is limited.

Climb up the Statue of Liberty

The Statue of Liberty

The Statue of Liberty is more than a monument. She is a beloved friend, a living symbol of freedom to millions around the world. These exhibits attribute to the people who created her, to those who built and paid for her, to the ideals she represents, and to the hopes she inspires.

Visitors can experience a special insider's view of the engineering marvel that is the Statue of Liberty. To better understand this monumental work of art, visitors can view inside the Statue through a glass ceiling, guided by a park ranger, an enhanced lighting and new video system. In addition, visitors can enjoy walking out onto the Statue's observation deck to see the panoramic views of New York City and the Harbor.

Observation at Empire State Building

Empire State Building

The building, one of New York City's main tourist attractions, offers a variety of activities for its visitors. One can tour the Observatory 365 days per year, day and night, rain or shine for breathtaking views of Manhattan and beyond. The famous movie, King Kong was filmed in this building.

Also, there are two restaurants, a sushi bar, three coffee shops, a drug store, a Hallmark card shop, a post office and two banks, in addition to the plethora of restaurants and nightlife activities in the surrounding area. Located on the 86th floor, 1,050 feet (320 meters) above the city's bustling streets, the Observatory offers panoramic views from within a glass enclosed pavilion and from the surrounding open-air promenade.

Monument by moon night

Washington DC's spectacular monuments at night are not to be missed. With stops at the Iwo Jima Memorial, FDR Memorial, Lincoln Memorial, Vietnam Veteran and Korean War Memorials you will definitely want to bring your camera. Washington, D.C. is most beautiful after the sun sets.

Lincoln Memorial

3.2 Food and Dining

Cooking in the US is not just hamburgers, pizza and fast food. The fast food restaurant chains have been very successful at introducing American style fast food around the world, now people from many lands believe it is what Americans all eat fast food. As the melting pot of many different cultures, the US has also become the mixing pot for many different cuisines, and it has a rich variety of foods to choose from.

American Hamburger

Regional cooking varies from state to state and is highly influenced by the types of ingredients locally available, as well as the cultural background of the people that settled in the area. New England cooking, native to the northeastern states; was heavily influenced by the cuisine of the original English settlers. Southern cooking has definite African influences. Cajun cooking, from the New Orleans area, is a spicy mixture of Spanish, French and African styles. California cooking is known for the use of fresh fruits and vegetables in interesting combinations with Asian, Mexican and Spanish flavorings.

Ethnic foods of all sorts are popular everywhere in the US and readily available in most areas. Italian cuisine is popular everywhere, from fast food pizza to gourmet Italian regional cuisine. The same is true of Chinese cuisine. Mexican restaurants are extremely popular in the southwestern and western states and can be found throughout the rest of the states as well. In most cities you will also find restaurants serving Eastern European, Greek, Middle Eastern, Indian, African, South American, Caribbean and numerous other cultural foods.

3.3 Shopping and Entertainment

Many tourists visiting the US on vacation enjoy shopping for bargains. American whiskey, fashion jeans, children's clothing, plush bath towels and fine bed linens are all popular items for shoppers from other countries. You can find many bargains in the US if you know where to shop and how to take advantage of the competitive sales.

Shoppers on the street

Sears and JC Penny's are two large national chains with stores across the US. They are similar to department stores but they do not offer high fashion merchandise or prestigious brands. Instead, they feature good quality merchandises at affordable prices. They are particularly known for their selection of children's clothing, home appliances, house wares and domestic goods. Sears is famous for its selection of tools and lawn and garden products.

Shopping mall in New York City

Outlet stores or factory outlets sell high quality merchandise with a well-known brand at discounted prices. They usually offer merchandise with slight manufacturing flaws and remainders from the last season or the previous year. They do not have end-of-season sales like the department stores, as their merchandise is always discounted 20% to 40% below department store prices. If you take advantage of the end-of-season sales at a department store, you can frequently get better bargains. At all other times, the outlet store is the best buy. Outlet malls with many hundreds of top brand name outlet stores like Levi's, Ralph Lauren, Timberland, and Pioneer can be found in most states, and they are often a bargain hunter's wonderland.

Discussion Questions

1. What activities would you like to try in the US?
2. When you are in Las Vegas, would you like to gamble?
3. Would you like to spend the vacation in Grand Canyon or New York City?
4. What kinds of souvenirs are you going to purchase in the US?
5. Are you going to enjoy American style food? What's your favorite?

Tips for Travelers

▣ USA Holidays

New Year's Day - January 1
Valentine's Day - February 14
St Patrick's Day - March 17
Easter - celebrated every year in March or April
Mother's Day - the 2nd Sunday in May
Fourth of July- July 4
Columbus Day - October 12
Halloween - October 31
Thanksgiving-the 4th Thursday of November
Christmas - December 25

English & Culture in Tourism

Chapter 5
Pacific Island I (Guam/Hawaii)

Australia
New Zealand
Canada
U.S.A.
Guam
Hawaii
the Northern Mariana Island

Chapter 5

Pacific Island I(Guam/Hawaii)

GETTING STARTED...

Guam

Location Oceania, island in the North Pacific Ocean, about three-quarters of the way from Hawaii to the Philippines

Climate Tropical marine; generally warm and humid, moderated by northeast trade winds; dry season from January to June, rainy season from July to December; little seasonal temperature variation

Ethnic Groups Chamorro 37.1%, Filipino 26.3%, other Pacific islander 11.3%, white 6.9%, other Asian 6.3%, other ethnic origin or race 2.3%, mixed 9.8%

Religions Roman Catholic 85%, other 15%

Languages English 38.3%, Chamorro 22.2%, Philippine languages 22.2%, other Pacific island languages 6.8%, Asian languages 7%, other languages 3.5%

Tumon beach, Guam

UNIT 1 About Pacific Island(Guam/Hawaii)

Grammar Focus

1. Auxiliary Verb - will

Will presents the future tense, subject's intention

Will always come with the original form of verb

You will experience

2. Passive preposition: by

A by B means B does something for A

You will experience the history by sampling of some foods.

Vocabulary

ancient	occupy
comprise	retain
approximately	rugged
lush	volcanic
terrain	coral
cliff	peak
lava	fuse
crater	shelter
medical	dwell
heritage	hew

Guam

Hafa Adai means hello. Guam has something for everyone. The unique Chamorro culture and language are a blend of Spanish, Micronesia, Asian and western influences over the last 300 years. You will experience the history and living traditions with a visit to the historic sites or by sampling some of delicious food.

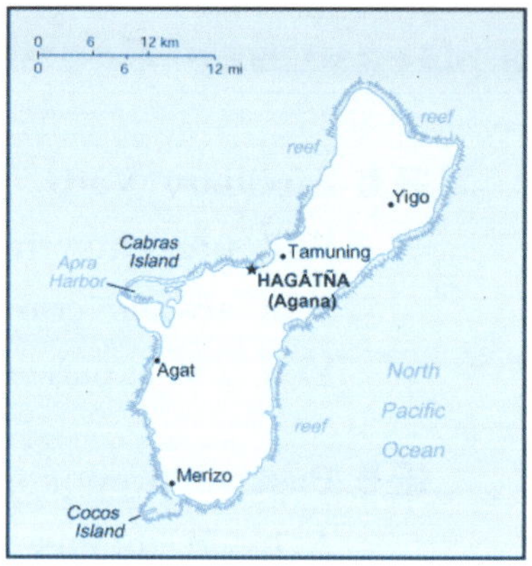

Map of Guam State

The name Guam comes from the ancient Chamorro word "Guahan," meaning "we have." The Chamorro people arrived on Guam from the Malay Peninsula around 3000 BC, and they occupied the island alone until Ferdinand Magellan landed there in 1521. Having survived invasions by the Spanish, the Japanese and the Americans, they still comprise 43 percent of the island's population, and they have managed to retain their cultural identity, including language, customs and cuisine.

Guam is located 13 degrees North latitude and 144 degrees East longitude, which translates in flight time to 3 hours west of Japan and 5 hours north of Australia. Guam's land area covers approximately 212 square miles. From the northern tip of the island to the southern tip is approximately 30 miles. Guam's width varies by location from 4 to 12 miles. The landscape of the island varies from a flat to a rugged and lush volcanic terrain in the south with several rivers, streams and waterfalls. Most of the island is surrounded by a coral barrier reef, while sandy beaches, mangroves, and rugged cliff line characterize the coastline.

The island was formed millions of years ago when a pair of volcanoes sank beneath the ocean leaving only their twin peaks above sea level. The lava remains of the southern volcano eventually fused with the older northern crater. This crater's limestone top had been formed underwater during a long period by an extensive coral polyp community.

There are more than 600 species of plants on Guam, of which 100 are trees. For generations, the Chamorro used plants to enhance their happiness, health, comfort, and safety. The spreading branches of iron wood and banyan trees provide shade from the midday sun and shelter from the wind. Many trees and smaller plants produce substances with medicinal qualities.

Most of Guam's life forms dwell in submerged areas offshore. Approximately 300 forms of rainbow hued hard coral and 50 soft coral inhabit Guam's reefs, and jewel-like tropical fish thrive in warm coastal waters.

In addition to its inviting beaches, elegant hotels, and great bargains, Guam has another vital attraction- its unique culture. The traditions and customs of Guam's proud island heritage thrive, despite invading conquerors, wars and epidemics, and changing governments.

Sunset, Tumon bay

Guam's traditional arts are very much alive. During cultural fairs and exhibitions, visitors often have the opportunity to watch master weavers, carvers even a blacksmith at works. Weavers, using the traditional pendants or coconut fibers, fashion baskets of various sizes, purses, hats, floor mats, and wall hangings. Carvers form the tables, plaques, figurines of people or animals, and household implements using Ifil mangrove, or pago woods.

Hawaii

Hawaii became the 49th state of the Unites States on August 21, 1959. During roughly 1778 - 1898, Hawaii was also known as the Sandwich Islands. Hawaii was first inhabited in roughly AD 1000, by foreign Polynesians who came from islands in the South Pacific, most likely the Marquesas. By colonizing Hawaii, these originally foreign settlers in effect became Hawaiian people.

Map of Hawaii

The kingdom established by Kamehameha lasted until 1893, when the last Hawaiian monarch, Liliuokalani, was overthrown in a coup led by wealthy American plantation owners and replaced by a Provisional Government, and later a Republic. During the kingdom and republic era, Hawaii's economy transitioned from that of an isolated state into that of a state integrated into the world's free market, producing and exporting more than two hundred thousand tons of sugar annually.

Hawaii is an ideal destination for swimming, tanning, surfing, boating, fishing, golf, and tropical exploration.

Sunset in Hawaii

Comprehension Check

1. The unique (   ) culture and language are a blend of Spanish, Micronesia, Asian and western influences over the last 300 years.

2. The name Guam comes from the ancient Chamorro word "Guahan," meaning (   )

3. The island was formed millions of years ago when a pair of (   ) sank beneath the ocean leaving only their twin peaks above sea level.

4. During roughly 1778~1898, Hawaii was also known as the (   ).

5. Hawaii is an ideal destination for (   ), tanning, (   ), boating, fishing, golf and (   ).

Discussion Questions

1. Have you ever been to Guam?

2. What is the reason that Guam has a blend culture with other countries?

3. What kind of cultural tradition does Guam have?

4. Where do you prefer to go on your honeymoon?

5. When is the best time to visit to Hawaii?

Useful Conversation

▣ When you travel, you have a chance to make a phone call to your acquaintance

A : Hello, is this Ms. Chang's house?

B : Yes, it is, but she is out now.

A : Do you know where she is now?

B : I don't know exactly, but maybe, I think she will be back in her office. Would you try to call her to the office?

A : Thanks for your advice. May I have her office number?

B : Yes, Wait a moment, will you hold on the line, please? I'll get it for you.

A : It's very kind of you

B : I'm sorry to have kept you waiting. Her office number is 555-2258

A : Thank you very much for your kindness

UNIT 2 Tourist Attractions

Grammar Focus

1. Agreement

The 3rd person singular noun has verb with －s / －es

The architectural design of the Government House incorporates elements of the Chamorro and Spanish cultural heritage.

2. Relative Clause, who

When an antecedent is a person, relative close combine with who

Honeymooners who visit this area ring the bell.

Vocabulary

historical	foundation
pillar	remains
architectural	residence
incorporate	command
entwine	vow
gleaming	shallow
reef	comprise
submerge	accomplished
quarry	installation

2.1 Guam-Agana

Government House

Adelupe Complex, Government House

The architectural design of the Government House - the Governor's official residence - incorporates elements of the Chamorro and Spanish cultural heritage. The building houses a mini-museum of Guam's antiquities. Located on Kasamata Hill in Agaña Heights, the residence commands an excellent view of Hagåtña and Agaña Bay. Construction on the original building began in 1952 and was completed two years later. Major reconstruction followed the destruction wrought by Super Typhoon Pamela in 1976, and the expanded structure occupies 22,000 square feet.

Two Lovers' Point (Puntan Dos Amantes)

Two lover's point

Legend holds that a pair of star-crossed Chamorro lovers whose parents would not allow them to marry jumped to their death from this 378-foot cliff. A giant statue of the entwined lovers is set on the top of a foundation. Honeymooners who visit this area ring the bell located on the top of the cliff, because couples believe that the ring makes their vow more faithful. Visitors have a splendid view from this point of the gleaming white-sand beaches and lush hillsides along the Philippine Sea in central Guam.

Tumon Bay

Tumon Bay

The tourist centre of Guam is just up the beach from Hagatña. Called Tumon Bay, it's essentially a one-road-deep resort strip fuelled by hotels, clubs and restaurants. Tumon Bay itself is quite shallow and at low tide, therefore it's possible to walk right out to the reef for a look around. Y'pao Beach Park is on the bay's southwest side and was once home to an ancient Chamorro village, as well as a leper and penal colony. These days it's a popular destination for travelers.

Underwater World

Underwater World

A visit to the Guam Aquarium Complex will take you on an attractive journey, fully submerged under 10 feet of water, inside a 7 foot wide, 7 foot tall, see-through acrylic tunnel. Along the way you will come nose to nose with sharks, rays, groupers, wrasse and other sea life, separated only by 3 inches of acrylic. You will experience scenes reserved for only the most accomplished diver, without ever getting wet. The tunnel dive will navigate you through various habitats as you find them near coast and off-shore in the depths of the Pacific Ocean.

Pago Bay

Pago River

This is the largest bay on the central windward side of the island, and one of Guam's most beautiful. A Spanish settlement near the mouth of the Pago River was wiped out by a small-pox epidemic in 1856. At the far end of the bay is the University of Guam's Marine Biology Laboratory, known internationally for its researc

An unmarked viewpoint just past the town of Yona on Guam's central eastern coast lets you gaze out over the Pago River as it empties into the broad Pago Bay. According to legend, a giant fish who wanted to cut the island in half at its narrowest point used to nibble away at the land here, but Guam was saved from bisection by a woman who wove her long hair into a net and scooped up the mischievous fish.

Latte Park

As early as 500 A.D. ancient Chamorros built their houses on stone pillars known as lattes. These pillars are notable for their two-piece construction; the supporting column (hala-gi) topped with a capstone (tasa). The halagi was made from coral limestone and usually carried several miles from the quarry site for installation in the appropriate location. The tasa was made from natural, coral heads collected from the reef. In Latte Park, eight of these stones are displayed. These lattes were transferred to their present location in Hagåtña from Me'pu, their original location in Guam's southern interior.

Latte Park

South Pacific Memorial Park

This peaceful park was the site of one of the bloodiest battles in the closing days of World War II. This was the site of the last Japanese garrison under the command of General Obata. In a desperate fight with American forces in 1944, General Obata was killed trying to maintain control of Guam. The park was set aside in memory of the more than half million Japanese soldiers as well as American soldiers and local people who lost their lives in the Pacific War between 1941 and 1945. It symbolizes the determination of the two nations to promote friendship and seek world peace. A 15 meter-high tower is a representation of hands praying for peace.

The Pacific National Historic Park

2.2 Hawaii

Kauai

The traditions of the many cultures that make up life on Kauai center around ohana (family). Children are not only welcomed; they're celebrated. This unique corner of the tropics is a virtual playground for children. Family-oriented accommodations, activities and restaurants make family trips safe, easy, fun and economical. The Kauai Children's Discovery Museum in Kapaa isn't just for children. Interactive exhibits, virtual reality games, and hands-on science and art activities will delight adults as well.

Kauai lagoons

On Saturdays, the Starlight Planetarium Program tells how the Polynesian voyagers used the stars, winds and ocean to navigate their canoes across the Pacific. Most of the major resorts on Kauai have programs for kids that include fun, educational activities like Hawaiian crafts and cultural activities, fishing, beach games, nature walks, surfing lessons, sand sculpture contests, coconut frond weaving, tide pool explorations, tours of historic sites, and fieldtrips led by local naturalists and other experts.

Oahu

In Hawaii, it's evident that caring for keiki (children) is very important. On Oahu, there are a variety of exciting activities designed specifically with kids and families in mind. Take a submarine ride and witness sunken ships, airliners and reef structures. Ride the thrilling waterslides at Hawaiian Waters Adventure Park. Get up close and personal with dolphins, sea turtles, stingrays, sharks, and moray eels at Sea Life Park. Spend the day at the Honolulu Zoo or Waikiki Aquarium and see animal and marine life like you've never seen anywhere else. Or explore 4,000-acres of fun at Kualoa Ranch by horse, ATV, helicopter, Jet Ski or kayak.

There are also plenty of other educational and cultural excursions for kids and families year-round, including nature walks, hikes, wildlife feedings, fishing, catamaran sails and more. Many hotels and condominiums also offer programs for kids that include activities such as lei and kite making, lauhala weaving, and sandcastle building.

Hanauma beach, Oahu

Maui

While famous around the world as an unforgettable honeymoon destination, Maui also offers an abundance of friendly attractions too.

Take a trek through a bamboo forest and scout for rare tropical birds.

Aerial view of Maui

Spend each day on a different beach. Hike down an ancient path, or straight up a volcano. Take a road trip to the other side of the island, or take a glass-bottom boat ride to a whole new world.

Several of the larger resort hotels provide supervised activity programs for guests, giving them a unique opportunity to experience Hawaii's culture.

Big Island

Hawaii's Big Island is a big ohana, and that means family, whether it's a traditional mom & dad and kids, blended, extended, multi generational family reunion or a group of old friends. The Big Island ohana embraces groups of people traveling together, of different ages, with different interests and tastes. And there's an adventure waiting for anyone with a sense of play and imagination.

In one day, visitors can experience the desert-like lava plains along the Kona coast and the rainiest city in America, Hilo. Go from sea level to the world's tallest mountain, Mauna Kea (13,796 when measured from sea level, 33,500 from the ocean floor), cruise through green rainforest or black lava rock. Watch whales, swim with dolphins, whisper to horses or listen to rare birdsong, sleep in the hotel industry's best, or camp out in seldom-seen places.

the north shore, Big Island

Comprehension Check

1. Honeymooners who visit this area ( ) located on the top of the cliff, because couples believe that the ring makes their vow more faithful.
2. Along the way you will come nose to nose with sharks, rays, groupers, wrasse and other ( ), separated only by 3 inches of acrylic.
3. The ( ) public market offers visitors a glimpse into the island's culture, lifestyle, and cuisine.
4. On ( ), the Starlight Planetarium Program tells how the ( ) voyagers used the stars, winds and ocean to navigate their canoes across the Pacific.
5. Hawaii's Big Island is a big ohana, and that means ( ), whether it's a traditional mom & dad and kids, blended, extended, multi generational ( ) reunion or a group of old friends.

Discussion Questions

1. When you are in Guam, which attractions would you like to visit first?
2. What is your feeling about the Pacific National Historic Park?
3. What kinds of activities do you like to do in Hawaii?
4. When you are in Hawaii, which islands would you like to visit?

Useful Conversation

▣ When you travel, you have to go to tourist information center.

A : Where can I get a map of the town and the subway lines?

B : Here you are, sir.

A : How much do I owe you?

B : It's free of charge, sir. This is hotel brochure for tour guide.

A : Thanks for your kindness. I'd like to take a look around the city this evening. Can I get a ticket for the sightseeing bus?

B : Yes, of course. What night tours do you want?

A : Can I see a timetable?

B : Sure, here it is.

A : I'd like to take tour 5th, where can I catch the bus?

B : You can take the bus in front of this hotel.

A : Thank you very much.

UNIT 3 Things to do

3.1 Amazing experience

Water sports

Water sports are, without a doubt, Guam's finest offering. Visitors who come to Guam to enjoy the island's ocean playground can choose from a full range of activities that will take them either over or under the surface of Guam's inviting tropical seas.

Sea kayaking

Jet ski, windsurfing, sea kayak, and other water-sports equipment, and lessons are available at some of the hotels. Several companies offer sport facilities in Tumon Beach, Cocos Island, Hagatña, and other parts of the island.

Water tours

Water tours are an instant escape from land activities. You can take riverboat trips with a group or paddle by yourself in a kayak.

Cruise, Agana Bay

Dolphin watching is a popular way of enjoying Guam's marine life to include seeing jumping spinner dolphins. A dive in a submarine will get you a close up look at the island's teeming fish and plant life. Or, try one of the two semi-submersible boats that can take you to some of the best marine sites around Guam.

Diving

Scuba diving and snorkeling are especially popular on Guam where more than 350 types of coral, vast numbers of fish, and submerged wrecks provide varied forms of entertainment. Popular snorkeling spots for beginners include the protected bays inside the reef at Tumon Bay, Piti Bomb Hole and Merizo. Well-equipped dive shops are located conveniently between Tumon and Agat. You can rent everything you need for diving, even a qualified dive instructor.

Golfing

Golf Course in Tourism

A round of golf in one of Guam's many golf courses is an opportunity well worth the effort. Several locations and course difficulties designed by such golfing greats as Jack Niklaus, Gary Player, and Sam Snead are spread throughout the island. A golf driving range, located close to Tumon, is open until 10:00 p.m. Golf clubs, shoes, and other equipment may be rented at the pro shop.

Dinner show

Dancers in Guam

Guam has several dinner shows that offer a variety of cultural dance troops. These dancers are some of the finest in the region and often win awards at annual competitions in Hawaii. In addition to many island-style performances, Guam also has a full-blown Las Vegas-style dinner show complete with world-class illusionists. Venue sites for these shows are varied as well, with some being dinner cruises and others being land bound. All shows serve plenty of food and drinks to keep their guest smiling.

Jungle River Tour

Ipan beach located in the Southern village of Talofofo is a great place for families, as the water has fewer rocky coral reefs. Also, there's a 30-minute jungle tour by a cruise boat that shows you the lush flora and fauna of the island while passing near a 600 year-old village of the native Chamorro tribes.

Jungle tour

Honolulu Lei Greeting

Start your Hawaii vacation off with Aloha. Arrange a traditional flower lei greeting for your arrival at the airport. Your friendly island greeter will welcome you with a warm "aloha" and offer you assistance to baggage claim or directions to your connecting inter-island flight.

Honolulu Zoo

The zoo is home to 1,230 mammals, birds & reptiles. Over 750,000 people visit the Honolulu Zoo annually. It is the largest zoo within a radius of 2,300 miles and unique in that it is the only zoo in the United States originating from a King's grant of royal lands to the people.

Honolulu Zoo

Hilo Tropical Garden

Nestled on land owned by the estate of one of Hawaii's last princesses, Hilo Tropical Gardens, established in 1948, is one of Hawaii Island's oldest visitor gardens.

Hilo Tropical Garden

3.2 Food and Dining

Guam

Guam is a heaven of the culinary arts. Despite Guam's small population, a wide array of restaurants offers splendid delicacies to warm any palate. Major hotels and restaurants serve quality Continental meals and exotic ethnic dishes, as well.

The traditional menu includes such favorites as Kadon Octopus (octopus stewed in coconut milk with onions and sweet peppers), Eskabeche (fresh fish marinated in vinegar and soy sauce) and Shrimp Kelaguen (minced shrimp mixed with lemon, onions, peppers and shredded coconut).

Guam's traditional menu

Travelers who venture further will find Chamorro, Japanese, Korean, Thai, Vietnamese, Filipino, Chinese, Mexican, and European restaurants, each with its own distinct environment. Of course, American fast food chains have become standard fare for those on the go. Guam also has several all-u-can-eat restaurants, many of which offer really good lunch buffet prices. Dinner buffets tend to be a little more costly.

Hawaii

Hawaii has always been linked with food - ever since Captain Cook named the Islands after his sponsor, the Earl of Sandwich. The various ethnic groups that immigrated to Hawaii in the last 200 years didn't forget their cook pots - filled with some of the most delectable aromas on earth.

The kaleidoscope of cultures that make up the peoples of the Islands allows you to experience the special diversity that is dining out in Hawaii. Hawaii's multi-ethnic convergence of cuisines is just like Hawaiian culture - a melting pot of tastes - offering so many worlds for the choosing.

3.3 Shopping and Entertainments

Chamorro Village in Guam

Centrally located along Hagåtña Bay, the cluster of shops is reminiscent of the old Spanish market. Fresh produce, the catch of the day, local handicrafts, and various curios surround stalls of eateries that serve international dishes. A main hall is used for occasional shows featuring local talent.

Shows in Chamorro Village

Flea market in Guam

For shoppers who rise with the sun, Guam's popular flea markets are a special treat. Every Saturday and Sunday morning at 6 a.m., the Dededo Flea Market, located on Marine Drive, welcomes throngs of bargain hunters with the intent of finding the best buys

Flea market in Guam

among rows and rows of new and used merchandise.

Buyers can find everything from lawn mowers to baby clothes, plants to pets. Hot snacks and beverages are available, and many people enjoy an island-style breakfast of fried rice, eggs and meat while shopping.

Aloha Festival

The Aloha Festivals is an annual series of free cultural celebrations observed in the state of Hawaii in the United States. It is the only statewide cultural festival in the nation. It features concerts, parades, street parties called ho'olaule'a as well as various other special events planned for resident and tourist families. The Aloha Festivals are celebrated on six islands — Kauai, Oahu, Maui, Molokai, Lanai, and the Big Island of Hawaii — over the course of six weeks in September and October.

Discussion Questions

1. Have you ever tried local taste when you were traveling? If so, what kind of food did you have?

2. Among the listed water activities, which do you want to try?

3. When you are shopping, would you prefer to shop in duty free or flea market?

Tips for Travelers

■ Big Summer Festival, July in Guam

Held annually during the summer months at Y'pao Beach Park, this is an Independence Day party with season-long implications, kicking off as it does the Guam Visitors Bureau's Summer Campaign to promote interest in Guam culture and tourism. Musicians and other entertainers representing many Micronesian and other Pacific countries perform. Vendors sell local foods, drinks and handicrafts. Parking is plentiful, and shuttles service most major area hotels. Admission is free.

Agahna, capital of Guam

Chapter 6
Pacific Island II
(The Northern Marianas Island, Saipan, Rota, Tinian)

Australia
New Zealand
Canada
U.S.A.
Guam
Hawaii
the Northern Mariana Island

Chapter 6

Pacific Island II
(The Northern Marianas Island, Saipan, Rota, Tinian)

GETTING STARTED...

Location Oceania, islands in the North Pacific Ocean, about three-quarters of the way from Hawaii to the Philippines

Climate Tropical marine; moderated by northeast trade winds, little seasonal temperature variation; dry season December to June, rainy season July to October

Ethnic Groups Asian 56.3%, Pacific islander 36.3%, Caucasian 1.8%, other 0.8%, mixed 4.8%

Religions Christian (Roman Catholic majority, although traditional beliefs and taboos may still be found)

Languages Philippine languages 24.4%, Chinese 23.4%, Chamorro 22.4%, English 10.8%, other Pacific island languages 9.5%, other 9.6%

Managana Bay, Saipan

UNIT 1 About the Northern Marianas Islands

Grammar Focus

1. Infinitive

To + the original form of Verb

The US used Tinian to stage air raids on Japan.

Gave the USA exclusive rights to administer them and to establish and maintain military bases.

2. Comparative degree

As + the positive degree + as

as unforgettable as

as well as

Vocabulary

hospitality
relaxation
spirit
ethnic
humidity
typhoon
hostility
invasion
devastated
contract
venture
plain
bustle
consistently
stuffy
indigenous
raid
unscathed
commonwealth

On three main islands of Saipan, Tinian and Rota, visitors experience the unhurried, friendly lifestyle and warm, island hospitality that are as unforgettable as the magical Micronesian sunsets. Via many convenient organized tours, or venturing out on your own, you can unlock the secrets of paradise. Relaxation, adventure, new cultural insights, and just plain fun, are treasures offered by a Northern Marianas Islands travel. Once you shared the unique island spirit, the tropical warmth will be yours forever.

The Northern Marianas, tropical paradise offers the relaxing shores of magnificent beaches and crystal clear blue waters, as well as the lively bustle of night life, shopping, a wide range of ethnic restaurants, and a variety of outdoor activities. It's also got its charms from turquoise waters, white sands, fine diving, snorkeling and hiking.

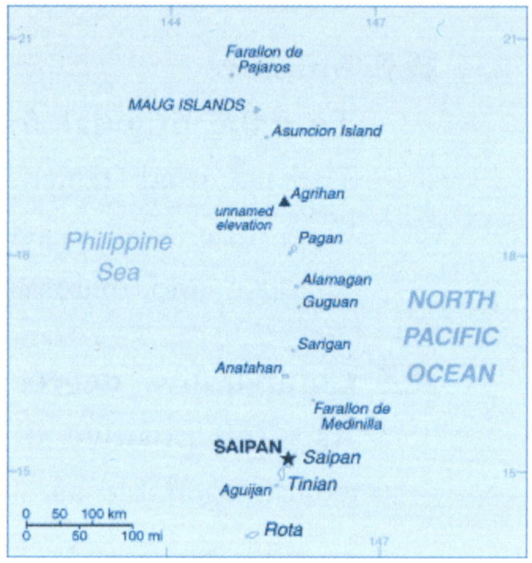

Map of the Northern Marianas Islands

This far western region of the Pacific consistently delivers temperatures between 20°C (68°F) and 30°C (86°F) at any time of the day, any day of the year. Humidity is always high but the even temperature and fresh sea breezes are never too stuffy. Rainfall is moderately heavy for most of the year but typhoons tend to pay the islands. It visits between July and November, and brings with heavy downpours.

The Northern Marianas were settled around 1500 BC by Chamorros who shared cultural ties with Guam's indigenous people. This early group of Chamorros is responsible for the 'latte stones' found throughout the

Marianas.

Ferdinand Magellan named the islands the Islas de los Ladrones (Islands of Thieves) in 1521 and the islands were renamed with Las Marianas upon the arrival of Spanish priest Luis Diego Sanvitores, in honor of the Spanish queen Maria Ana of Austria. In 1668, Sanvitores and five other priests established the first mission in the Marianas, touching off two decades of hostilities between the priests and less-than-welcoming Chamorros.

The Spanish relocated most of the Chamorros to Guam. Most of the natives on Rota, however, managed to hide out in the hills and avoid capture, and today the Chamorros on Rota are the least mixed in the Marianas.

Around 1820, the Spanish allowed islanders from the western Carolines to move to the larger Mariana Islands. The Carolinians managed Spanish cattle herds and maintained a presence in the Marianas at a time when Spain was concerned over German intentions in the area.

The US used Tinian to stage air raids on Japan, including the atomic bomb drops on Hiroshima and Nagasaki. Bypassed by the US invasion forces, Rota came out of the war relatively unscathed; Saipan and Tinian, though, were devastated. The United Nations made the Marianas a department of the Trust Territory of the Pacific Islands in 1947 and gave the US exclusive rights to administer them and to establish and maintain military bases (and to prevent other countries from doing the same).

When the CIA moved out of Saipan in 1962, the Northern Marianas were finally opened to visitors. The people of the Northern Marianas voted to become a US commonwealth in 1975, ensuring continued the US economic support. In 1986 a new commonwealth contract became effective, granting islanders US citizenship.

Comprehension Check

1. This far western region of the Pacific consistently delivers temperatures between (   ) at any time of the day, any day of the year.

2. The Northern Marianas were settled around 1500 BC by (   ) who shared cultural ties with Guam's indigenous people.

3. In 1668, Sanvitores and five other (   ) established the first mission in the Marianas.

4. The US used Tinian to stage (   ) on Japan, including the atomic bomb drops on Hiroshima and Nagasaki.

5. In 1986 a new (   ) contract became effective, granting islanders US citizenship.

Discussion Questions

1. Have you ever been to Saipan or any other lands in the Northern Marianas Islands?

2. If you have time, would you like to visit these islands?

3. Where is your preferable island among three islands?

4. Do you know any other island which is Commonwealth of the US?

Useful Conversation

▣ When you travel, you will have a chance to take a local transportation

A : When does the bus leave?

B : Every twenty minutes until ten o'clock.

A : How much is it?

B : Two dollars.

A : Does the bus go to near Time Square?

B : Yes, it does, but you have to transfer.

A : Where I have to change the bus?

B : You have to get off Central Station and then take the subway Green line.

A : How long does it take?

B : It takes about thirty minuets.

A : Thanks a lot.

UNIT 2 Tourist Attractions

Grammar Focus

1. Gerund : V + ing = Noun

A popular local picnic area and jogging trail in central Saipan is the beautifully landscaped American Memorial Park.

2. Ordering : Adverb + Adjective + Noun

the beautifully landscaped American Memorial Park

Vocabulary

spectacular	breathtaking
cannon	relics
fortress	stroll
memorials	dedicated
accessible	renovated
girdled	poetically
artillery	barge
surrender	surge
roar	observation
elevation	summit

2.1 Saipan

Northern Saipan is rich in spectacular natural beauty and historical landmarks. Islan Maigo Fahang (Bird Island) is a must see with its breathtaking view of an isolated emerald bay. Explore Banadero Cave's (Last Command Post) World War II tanks, cannons, war relics, and natural limestone cave fortress.

Enjoy panoramic views from high on the top Laderan Banadero (Suicide Cliff) and sheer sea cliffs at Puntan Sabaneta (Banzai Cliff). Take a cool swim in the Grotto, a huge limestone cavern connected to the open ocean by underwater passages - a super thrill for advanced scuba divers. Take a stroll of bike down the Marpi Pathway and visit the many peace memorials dedicated to the soldiers and families who gave their lives during World War II.

Downtown, Saipan

A popular local picnic area and jogging trail in central Saipan is the beautifully landscaped American Memorial Park. A trip to Saipan would not be complete without a visit to the original Managaha Island, easily accessible for day trips by speed boats.

Botanical Garden, Saipan

Mount Tapochau, the highest point on Saipan, offers a 360-degree view of the island. Renovated from an old Japanese Hospital, the CNMI Museum of History and Culture is featuring the exhibits and displays of life in the Marianas before modern times.

While cruising in the southern part of the island, stop and stroll at the Beach Road Pathway, a perfect spot to enjoy one of our magnificent sunsets. Plan to spend a day exploring the hundreds of exotic tropical flora at the award-winning Saipan Botanical Garden.

Bird Island

Bird Island is located on the northern part of the island. It is a small cliff-girdled island, and the Japanese more poetically called Moon Viewing Island.

Bird Island

Managana Island

Beautiful Managana Island, in the Tanapag is the most popular snorkeling site on Saipan. A white sandy beach runs right along Managana, which was captured from the Japanese only after the main island had fallen. Three Japanese artillery pieces are still there, and a great array of sunken barges, landing craft, ships, planes, and guns can be seen among the coral heads near the island, on the sandy bottom in only 6 to 12 meters of water

Managana Island

Suicide Cliff

Just above the Okinawa Peace Memorial is Suicide Cliff. From this high post hundreds of Japanese soldiers jumped 250 meters to their deaths rather than surrender to the US Forces.

Suicide Cliff

Grotto

The Grotto is a beautiful sunken pool connected to the sea by underwater passages. The sunlight shining on the ocean outside the cavern gives the water its deep blue color during the day. Be careful of the powerful surge of water roaring back and forth into the Grotto. Do not swim out into the ocean as it may be difficult to return.

Mt. Tapochau

For the best scenic views of Saipan, follow the signs on Capitol Hill and take a drive up to the island's highest point, Mount Tapochao. Enjoy the complete 360-view of the whole island from Marpi to San Antonio, and if you're lucky you can see Tinian and Aguiguan (Goat Island). A favorite time to visit Mt. Tapochao is during the sunset, when the ocean, clouds and sky change colors right before your eyes.

Mt. Tapochau

The capture of Mt. Tapochao on June 25, 1944 gave the US Marines the advantage of superior ground observation and permitted the Americans to look down on Japanese positions. The elevation is 1,545 feet (515 meters). The entire island can be seen from its summit.

2.2 Tinian

This sleepy one-village island, just 2km south of Saipan, has escaped major tourism development and makes a good escape if Saipan's bustle gets to be too much. It's hard to imagine that such a peaceful place could have been involved in one of the most violent events in history.

Near the Tinian Harbor, check out the gigantic, hand-carved limestone latte stones at the House of Taga, home of Tinian's legendary Chief Taga. The northern end of the island is home to the sprawling North Field and numerous World War II structures such as the Atomic Bomb Pits.

While up north, experience the awesome poser and beauty of nature at the Blow Holes. In the central part of the island, get a scenic view of the island at Mount Lasso. In the south, peers over the steep cliffs pound waves at Suicide Cliff.

Atomic Bomb Pits

From an ominous spot on this airfield, a pit slightly larger than a grave and similarly covered over with flowering plants is the site where the world's first atomic bomb to be later exploded in anger and lifted into the belly of a B-29 Super fortress.

At No. 1 Bomb Loading Pit the atomic bomb was loaded aboard an American B-29 called Enola Gay on the afternoon of August 5, 1945, to be dropped on Hiroshima the next day. At nearby No. 2 Bomb Loading Pit a second atomic bomb was loaded on August 9, 1945 and dropped on Nagasaki On August 10, 1945, Emperor Hirohito decided to end the Pacific war without his cabinet's consent.

House of Taga

Pacific Islanders have always had some mysterious attraction for monoliths. It is as if these ancient people wanted to leave for future generations. Their stone proves that it could stand before the withering effect of the centuries with their illegible message in stone.

Taga stones

The Taga Stones may be such an example of a strange, unpredictable need to use enduring limestone for some unknown purpose. The precise use of these huge pillars, cut from solid rock or reef coral, remains a mystery. Some believe that they may have been the foundation for large elevated structures, temples or meeting houses such as the House of Taga.

Blow Holes

For an awesome display of one of Mother Nature's wonders, people visit the spectacular blow holes on Tinian's northeast coast. You can walk over the sharp rocks right up to the blow holes, which are carved out of the coral rock by the powerful wave action. When the waves are big the water shooting

Blow hole on Tinian Coast

out of the blow holes can blast up to 10 meters in the air. Just a 45 minute ferry ride or five minutes by small, twin-engine plane, the island of Tinian offers quite a number of interesting attractions.

Taga Beach

Taga Beach is just a five-minute walk from the Tinian Dynasty Hotel. Great swimming, turquoise waters and white sand make this the perfect relaxation spot. Beautiful picnic areas, showers and Jet Ski rentals are available.

Taga Beach

2.3 Rota

The beautiful island of Rota possesses a unique character and charm that wins over just about everyone that goes there. On the western side of the island, take a refreshing swim in the cool, clear water at Rota's famous Swimming Hole. Just north of the airport, discover how the ancient Chamorros carved giant latte stones out of the limestone rock at the Taga Stone Quarry.

Further down the road, marvel at the thousands of seabirds that make their home at the Sagua'gaga Seabird Sanctuary. Learn more about the local culture and dozens of indigenous plant species at Taisacana's Botanical & Nature Trail. Check out the fascinating collection of artifacts at the Rota Cave Museum, located inside a giant limestone cavern.

At the entrance to Songsong Village, stop by Pinatang Park, a seawater park with numerous channels out to the open sea. Once in the village visit the Tonga Cave, a huge natural cavern with dozens of stalactites, stalagmites, tunnels, and mini caves.

Bird Sanctuary

At the Sagua'gaga Bird Sanctuary, seabirds nest at the base of the cliffs. Paths along the cliff edge overlook the nesting area and ocean.

Taga Stone Quarry

The Taga Latte Stones are mysterious column and pillar carving created by ancient Chamorros. Taga Stone Quarry is the only latte stone quarry in Micronesia.

stone quarry

Tweksberry Beach

Close to Songsong Village, Tweksberry beach and park are popular picnic and swimming areas on Rota. Crystal blue waters and white coral sand make this the perfect vacation spot. Take some great photos at Tweksberry Park with its perfectly lined rows of coconut palms. Continue east along beautiful Sasanhaya Bay and get a great view of Mt. Tapingot (Wedding Cake Mt.), and the two well-preserved Japanese Cannons.

Mt. Wedding cake

Comprehension Check

1. ( ) is located on the northern part of the island. It is a small cliff-girdled island, and the Japanese more poetically called Moon Viewing Island.

2. Beautiful ( ), in the Tanapag is the most popular snorkeling site on Saipan.

3. Just above the Okinawa Peace Memorial is ( ) Cliff.

4. The precise use of these huge pillars, hewn from solid rock or reef coral, remains a ( ).

5. When the waves are big the water shooting out of the ( ) can blast up to 10 meters in the air.

6. Taga Stone Quarry is the ( ) latte stone quarry in Micronesia.

Discussion Questions

1. What kind of mysterious story does this island have?

2. Which attraction is your favorite? Where will you spend your most time?

3. Do know how Chamorro people move the latte stone from the quarry to the historical site?

4. When you have a chance to visit to the Northern Marianas Islands, what kind of transportations will you take? Do you prefer to rent a car, or take a walk?

Useful Conversation

▣ When you travel, you need to ask the tip for travel.

A : Can you recommend sightseeing tour?

B : Is this your first visit to New York?

A : Yes, it is.

B : I'd like to recommend a sightseeing tour of the Statue of Liberty.

A : Where is it? I'd like to go there.

B : It is located in the southern end of New York City.

A : Would you tell me about Statue of Liberty?

B : It used to be the immigration center for all visitors and immigrants to America. But now it is a museum and stands for America.

A : I'll definitely go and see it.

B : That's great idea. I'll take you there.

A : Is it too far from here?

B : It takes about twenty minutes by the ferry

A : Ok, let's go there now.

UNIT 3 Things to do

3.1 Amazing Experience

A vacation is a time to get away from the hustle and bustle of the city and breathe in fresh air and sunshine. A vacation in a tropical paradise allows making images of sandy beaches, water sports, golf, and touring. And the Mariana Islands have all of those to offer. But that's not all. From morning until long after the sun goes down, all year round, the Mariana Islands provides visitors with exciting, and fulfilling things to do.

Managana Tour

The pearl of Saipan, "Managana Island" situated in the lagoon, lies 10 minutes by boat from the boat dock, offers a great beach and snorkel experience. A must visit site when visiting the islands.

Windsurfing

The gentle trade winds that blow the surface of the ocean offer ideal conditions for windsurfers. It enables you to enjoy windsurfing all year around in Saipan and from November to April is the best time to go due to the gentle breezes from South East Ocean.

Snorkeling

Snorkeling is an ocean sport where you can enjoy all of the fantastic scenery viewing the bottom from the top. Snorkeling allows you to float above the water while breathing through an apparatus inhaling air directly from above, while scuba allows you to go in deeper depths with a breathing apparatus on your back.

Snorkeling in the water

You can have free rentals of all equipment if you participate in one of the many snorkeling tours. Otherwise, you are able to rent from dive shops located nearby the beach.

Parasailing

Enjoy the panoramic view from the ocean as a parachute. It is hooked on a boat and takes you to on a ride approximately 30 meters high. It's an enjoyable experience overlooking the lagoon.

Parasailing, Managana Island

Sea Walker

View the underwater world by sea walking. Enjoy the various tropical fish that enhance your visit in a 3 meter deep dive. Visitors enjoy this popular adventure as they experience the underwater world commonly seen by certified divers only. Sea Walker is a safe and fun activity to enjoy.

Submarine Tour

An underwater adventure takes you aboard a real submarine. Take this fascinating 45-minute underwater adventure down 30 meters in the lagoon of Saipan and view the spectacular underwater world. A great tour for the family to enjoy the magnificent coral formations and various tropical fish makes an event to remember.

Spa treatment

Visitors looking to satisfy themselves will find a selection of spas to complete their every desire. Inspired by the natural beauty of the islands, the spas in the Mariana Islands offer a vacation within a vacation. From the most relaxing spa treatments come a rejuvenated mind, body, and spirit.

3.2 Food and Dining

Local specialties include kelaguin, a chewy mixture of diced chicken and shredded coconut and thin slices of raw coconut dipped in a peppery sauce. A wide choice of food is on offer, including Chinese, French, Italian, Japanese, Thai and the US.

From high class cuisine to hot pizza, from the Far East to the Wild West, Saipan has more restaurants than you can shake a fork at. Because of its unique geographical location

kelaguin

and ethnic mix, Saipan combines the best of Eastern taste with Western flavor spiced with local ingredients. Chamorro, Carolinian, American, Japanese, Chinese, Korean, Filipino, Italian, Mexican, Cajun, Thai, and Indian are just some of the tastes you'll find in Saipan's many restaurants.

3.3 Shopping and Entertainment

The Mariana Islands includes traditional Chamorro and Carolinian handicrafts and accessories made of gold, jade, coral and pearls.

Places to shop in Saipan

The LA Tax Free Shop offers a large selection of quality products. All products are displayed for a convenient and comfortable shopping experience. Its selection includes traditional Chamorro handicrafts, watches, liquors, cosmetics, leather products, electronics, and health & beauty products at the best prices possible.

The Hafa Adai Shopping Center is conveniently located beside the Hafa Adai Hotel and across the street from DFS Galleria. As a huge shopping venue, its selection includes a large supermarket, golf shop, the latest trendy fashion shops, a shoe shop, folk handicrafts shops and a food court.

Shopping in Rota

The specialty shop is located in Rota Powpow Hotel, and Cononut Village. The best selling product is Bojobo doll made with wood. Papaya jam and black pepper is also available.

Gambling in Tinian

Tinian Dynasty Hotel

From a turn of a card, to a spin of a wheel, gambling is available in Tinian at the Tinian Dynasty Hotel and Casino. This elegant 75,000 square foot casino offers an array of gaming action from the winning sounds of hundreds of slot machines to the classic game of Baccarat, Roulette, Craps, Pacific Poler, Black Jack as well as the popular Asian game, Sic Bo.

Discussion Questions

1. How can you identify yourself? Are you adventure lover or not?
2. Are you willing to meet sea creatures under the water?
3. Which activities would you like to try in this island?
4. Do you prefer to eat local delicacy? Where do you want for dinner? Local restaurant or hotel dinner show?

Tips for Travelers

▣ Annual Fiestas

Most villages have an annual fiesta in honour of their patron saint. Rota and Tinian each have one fiesta, while Saipan has six.
The largest and most popular fiesta in the Northern Marianas, however, is held on Rota on either the first or second weekend in October. The celebration, which honors San Francisco de Borja, includes a luau-like feast of Chamorro food, religious processions, music and dancing. Visitors are welcome at these annual festivals.

Festival, Rota

References

성명희. (2004). Practical Tourism English Reading 실용관광영어강독. 백산출판사.

성명희, 신영수 외. (2004). Guided Tourism English. 골든윙스.

월터 딕, 루 캐리 공저, 최수영 백영균 외 공역. (2003). 체계적 교수 설계. 아카데미프레스.

조웅래. (2002). Global Hotel English Conversation. 한올 출판사.

함영덕. (2001). Practical & Tourism English 생활관광영어. 백산출판사.

Brown, H.D. (2001). Teaching by Principles; an interactive approach to language pedagogy. New York, Longman

Ellis, R. (2000). Task-based Language Learning and Teaching. Oxford.

Freeman, D. (2000). Techniques and Principle in Language Teaching. Oxford.

Lightbown, P., M & Spada, N. (1999). How languages are learned. Oxford.

Murcia M., C. (2001). Teaching English as a Second or Foreign Language. Heinle & Heinle.

Nunan, D. (1998). Language Teaching methodology. Printice Hall.

Referential website

www.australia.com

www.newzealand.com

www.canada.com

www.nationalgeograhpic.com

www.startour.pe.kr

www.space.australia.com

www.cia.gov/cia/publications/factbook/index.html

www.hawaii.com

www.usatourist.com

www.janeresture.com/saipan/

www.visitguam.org

www.guampdn.com

www.travelnotes.org

www.hankooki.com

Profile of Authors

Myeong Hee Seong

Ph.D	Korea University
Head	Institute of Foreign Language Education, Eulji University
Professor	Dept. of Tourism & Management, Eulji University
Vice-President	Modern English Education Society
Director	Pan-Pacific Association of Applied Linguistics

Hyung-ji Chang

Ph.D. Candidate	Korea University
Master of Art	TESOL at Long Island University, U.S.A.
Adjunct Professor	Catholic University of Daegu
Edition Director	The Modern English Education Society
Director	Public Relation in Pan-Pacific Association of Applied Linguistics